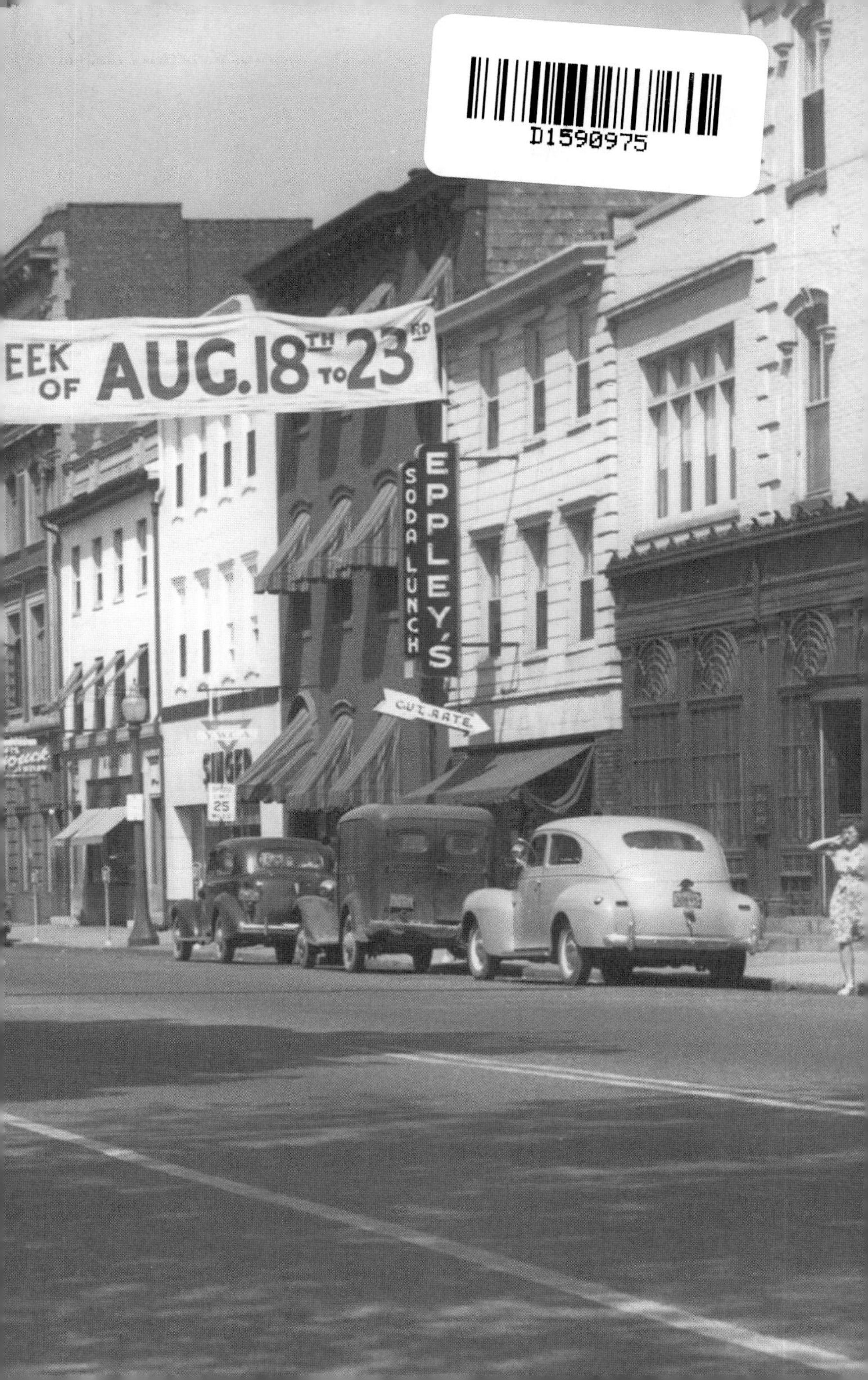
EEK OF AUG. 18TH TO 23RD
EPPLEY'S
SODA LUNCH
CUT RATE
Y.W.C.A
SINGER
25

ERNEST C. REISINGER

A Biography

Ernest Reisinger leaving Brown's Hotel after a visit to London in the 1960s.

ERNEST C. REISINGER

A Biography

GEOFFREY THOMAS

THE BANNER OF TRUTH TRUST

THE BANNER OF TRUTH TRUST
3 Murrayfield Road, Edinburgh EH12 6EL, UK
P. O. Box 621, Carlisle, PA 17013, USA

*

ISBN 0 85151 825 7

*

Printed and bound in Great Britain
at the University Press,
Cambridge

DEDICATED TO
WALTER AND JOIE CHANTRY
TOM AND MARGARET NETTLES
TOM AND DONNA ASCOL

CONTENTS

ACKNOWLEDGEMENTS

For my name to be given as the sole author of this biography of Ernest C. Reisinger is a little misleading. Ernie himself gathered much material in the form of remembrances and correspondence, and in that enterprise he was assisted by the invaluable labours of Katie Irwin, who researched, interviewed people for information, and read many letters. Matthew Allen helped to reorganize and edit the original material. Mack M. Tomlinson and Carol Brandt encouraged Ernie to complete it. I came in at the end of this process, inheriting those endeavours. How pleasant a task was mine. I am much indebted to all the above, and to Philip Craig and Iain Murray who read the manuscript and made many suggestions. But the final judgments have been mine and I take responsibility for them.

I am grateful to the Banner of Truth for approaching me and inviting me to write this. I have known Ernie since he spoke at a students' meeting at Westminster Theological Seminary in 1963. The book was a trust the Banner of Truth placed in me concerning the life of their oldest trustee. I consider it an honour to have opened a window for many people on the life of a significant personality in American evangelical

Christianity. What a fascinating period in its history have the decades of the lifetime of Ernest Reisinger been.

To complete this book needed some golden hours spent with the Reisingers (Ernie, Mima, Don and Barbara), in Cape Coral, Florida, where I scribbled down more of Ernie's insights. I wish I could have stopped every conversation and taken out my notebook whenever he said something that tickled me, such as, 'He had a brick less than a load', and 'Don't jump out of a tree until you know where you are going to land.' We ate and laughed together, sharing the same friends and convictions and possessed by the same longings. We also prayed much that God would be glorified by these chapters. I have been edified by his life story, in seeing what God has been pleased to do through an imperfect man. I long for others to know it too. Let the facts speak for themselves.

Don Reisinger is a special friend. We were born within a few weeks of one another, and one of the best things that has come out of my visits to Cape Coral has been getting to know him and Barbara better.

Writing the book has been a means of growth. I think the life described has given me aspirations towards becoming a more faithful witness in the world to my Lord and Saviour Jesus Christ. That is my longing for all who will read it.

GEOFF THOMAS
April 2002

1

CARLISLE, PENNSYLVANIA

THE PRETTY TOWN OF CARLISLE lies in south-central Pennsylvania. It is located one hundred and twenty miles west of Philadelphia, which itself borders on the states of New Jersey and Delaware, and it is about two hundred and forty miles from Pittsburgh, which is near Ohio and West Virginia on the western side of the state. Carlisle has a population of 30,000 people, and is set in Cumberland County, a region full of farmhouses, pastures and small towns, where Amish people are often seen in their distinctive clothing, riding along country roads in horse-drawn buggies. The rivers and creeks of Cumberland County teem with trout, bass, pickerel and walleyes. Near Carlisle is the 969-acre Pine Grove Furnace Park, with lakes for boating and swimming, lined with many campsites. Hikers can enjoy walking along a stretch of the Appalachian Trail, while lovers of music – especially brass bands – are catered for by an annual Arts Festival.

Founded in 1751, Carlisle was George Washington's choice for the Continental Army's first arsenal and school. It is the home of Dickinson College, the first place of learning chartered after the colonies became the United States of America. It was established, in the words of Benjamin Rush, one of its founders, as 'a college for the education of youth in the learned and foreign languages, the useful arts, sciences and literature'. Today it has about two thousand students, who can choose from thirty-five major areas of study. Its law school has a national reputation.

For many years Carlisle was the site of the Indian Industrial School where, from 1903 to 1912, the famous athlete James Francis Thorpe studied. A Sac (Sauk) and Fox Indian, Thorpe won gold medals in the pentathlon and decathlon in the 1912 Olympic Games in Sweden. He went on to excel in other major sports, both as an amateur and as a professional. In football, he became the founding father of the professional game and served as the first President of what became the National Football League. In baseball, Thorpe played with the New York Giants, Cincinatti Reds and Boston Braves. In 1950 he was judged America's Greatest All-Round Male Athlete.

The gold medals awarded to Jim Thorpe were controversially stripped from him by the International Olympic Committee in an over-zealous decision when it was learned that he had played semi-professional baseball at the Carlisle Indian Industrial School prior to his Olympic participation. His daughter fought for many years to get the Committee to return the medals, and it finally did so in 1982. A popular film was made of his life.

Prior to 1730 the whole of the Cumberland Valley west of the Susquehanna River belonged to the Indians. A trader, James Letort, son of French Huguenot parents, had a trading post for Indians at what is now Carlisle. In the 1730s and '40s immigrants from Scotland and Ireland, who were mainly

Presbyterians, moved to the region. They began farming and planted churches. Many a farmhouse had a Bible, the *Shorter Catechism*, Thomas Boston's *Human Nature in Its Fourfold State,* and *The Pilgrim's Progress*. The Welsh immigrants tended to congregate in the north of Pennsylvania in the coal and slate mining region around Scranton and Wilkes-Barre where they planted their Calvinistic Methodist churches. Near Carlisle some years ago, the author bought from an antiquarian book shop a Welsh translation of the Westminster *Shorter Catechism*, something he had never come across in Wales itself. In the second half of the eighteenth century, Lutheran and German Reformed settlers moved into Cumberland County. It was the Presbyterians of Carlisle who, before the Revolutionary War, started the school now known as Dickinson College. At the start of the nineteenth century the places of worship in the town consisted of a Presbyterian church, an Episcopal church, a Lutheran church and a German Reformed congregation.

During the early nineteenth century, Methodist circuit riders made their visits to the region and established churches. Later in the century, Anabaptists (Brethren) moved into the region and the Church of God (Pietists) emerged out of the Lutheran churches. The only Presbyterian church in Carlisle stood in the 'Old School' tradition. The tens of thousands of Scotsmen who had moved to Pennsylvania were accustomed to psalm-singing and the theology of the Westminster Confession of Faith. However, that congregation called George Duffield (later the author of 'Stand up! Stand up for Jesus') and in 1815 he began his controversial ministry at First Presbyterian Church. As his pastorate progressed, his theology came under the influence of Nathaniel W. Taylor of New Haven, Connecticut, a Congregational minister, the first incumbent of the Dwight Professorship of Didactic Theology at Yale Divinity School. Taylor rejected such biblical teaching as that the human race was blighted by original sin. He said, 'There is no such thing as sinning without walking.' In other words, sin is in the sinning, rather than in the nature, of every person. He believed that mankind had the natural power to choose not to sin.

By 1833, George Duffield was convicted by the Carlisle Presbytery of doctrinal infidelity to the Westminster Confession of Faith in a number of areas, yet he remained pastor of the church. Lyman Beecher and Albert Barnes were similarly charged, but acquitted during the same period. Protesting against their preacher's 'New England theology', seventy-six members left to form the Second Presbyterian Church, Carlisle, and to uphold 'Old School' theology.

During this very controversy, a young man was born and raised in Newville, which is ten miles from Carlisle. He graduated from Dickinson College in Carlisle (where other young Presbyterians studied in preparation for ministry) and proceeded from there to Princeton. In 1842, he was ordained as pastor of the Second Presbyterian Church in Carlisle. He was none other than T. V. Moore whose commentaries on several of the minor prophets and whose book entitled *The Last Days of Jesus* were all reprinted by the Banner of Truth Trust in the closing decades of the twentieth century. Moore ministered for only three years at Carlisle but established a Puritan library at Second Church, a number of whose volumes came into the possession of the pastor of Grace Baptist Church, Carlisle, one hundred and thirty years later.

The Civil War devastated the religious life of the United States. Carlisle felt the effects of the war. The famous battle at Gettysburg took place only 30 miles from the town. Deep theological divisions splintered every denomination, and the Old School Presbyterians lost their strength, their numbers dividing between Northern and Southern churches. Following the war, Old School and New School Presbyterians in the North reunited but without resolving fundamental theological differences. Then, at the end of the nineteenth century, the full impact of social Darwinism and Higher Criticism of the Bible began to strike home.

The heart of the resistance to the rise of modernism was found at the prestigious Princeton Seminary in New Jersey. Its history from 1812 has been movingly told in two volumes by Dr David B. Calhoun (*The History of Princeton Seminary*, Banner of Truth, 1994–6). Liberals within the United Presbyterian Church sought to capture that citadel, and the conservative professor leading the opposition to them was Dr B. B. Warfield.

After he died in 1921 the mantle of his leadership for the 'Princeton Theology' fell upon the shoulders of Dr J. Gresham Machen. He was amongst the greatest of Christian leaders in the first half of the twentieth century. Deservedly, all his books are still in print. Machen taught New Testament at Princeton Seminary from 1906 to 1929. He was considered the most popular lecturer on campus. Unfortunately, after a long power struggle, a new president was appointed who was committed to dismantling the historic Christian position of the school. For years he steadily worked until that goal was achieved and men unsympathetic with the theology of the Westminster Confession began to be invited to become teachers at Princeton.

Dr Machen and a number of other professors resigned from Princeton in 1929 and founded Westminster Theological Seminary in Philadelphia. There Machen gathered around him a faculty of the most stirring teachers, authors, exegetes and family men. They were God-fearing and devout men whose influence over generations of ministerial students proved to be immense. What a privilege for a young man to be taught by men like Cornelius Van Til, John Murray, Edward J. Young and Ned B. Stonehouse (Machen's biographer). When Machen sought to maintain the orthodoxy of the missionaries sent out and supported by the denomination he was put on trial by the United Presbyterian Church USA, forbidden to defend himself by appealing to the actual beliefs of those missionaries and suspended from the ministry. So a new denomination was started in 1936 by those who were outraged at the injustices perpetrated by liberalism, the Orthodox Presbyterian Church. The strife Machen had experienced weakened him physically, so that he succumbed to an attack of pleurisy in the winter of 1936 and died in a hospital in Bismarck, North Dakota, in January 1937.

These memorable events affected the churches of Carlisle for the remainder of the twentieth century. Robert S. Marsden, a Presbyterian minister in Middletown, seceded from the United Presbyterian Church along with Dr Machen and formed an OPC congregation. Middletown lies across the Susquehanna River from Carlisle. Robert Marsden's son George attended Westminster Seminary and became a noted church historian. The Second Presbyterian Church in Carlisle, formed to oppose New England theology a century earlier, still had some conservative members who were sympathetic with Machen's fight for historic Christianity, and they kept in touch with Robert Marsden. These people, though not their pastor, met for many years to pray for the cause of the gospel in Carlisle. They started a mission called Biddle Chapel to reach out to the lost in that community.

2

THE REISINGER FAMILY

THE NAME 'REISINGER' IS OF GERMAN ORIGIN and people of that name were among the early settlers in Pennsylvania. A Peter Reisinger served as a private in the York County Militia during the Revolutionary War. Born in Germany, he died in York County, America, in 1801. An Isaac Reisinger was a tax-collector in Carlisle who died in 1878. Another Reisinger, one Lewis, came from Liverpool, Pennsylvania. He hailed from Perry County (which is not far from Carlisle) and served as a private in the Civil War in the 173rd Regiment of Pennsylvania. A number of Reisingers served with the American troops during the First World War.

One of the most successful Reisingers was a certain Hugo from New York who received international recognition as a merchant and art collector in New York City. Born in Wiesbaden, Germany, he became one of the largest importers of general merchandise in America. His collection of modern paintings was considered one of the finest in the nation. He died in 1914.

At the other end of the social scale were a hard-working German farmer and his wife named Howard and Sarah

Reisinger. They had three sons, one of whom, Ernest Gilbert Reisinger, began his working life with the Pennsylvania Railroad. He married Cordelia Weller Forney in Harrisburg in 1918 and a year later their first child, also named Ernest, was born. Another two sons, Donald and John, were born, then a daughter, Grace Esther.

The Reisingers lived in humble circumstances in the backwoods of Perry County, Pennsylvania from 1924. That county was one of the poorest in the state. Ernie's schooling took place in a one-room schoolhouse with a single teacher in charge of a classroom of children ranging in age from five to thirteen. A pot-belly stove provided heat on freezing winter days, and the toilets were primitive. The walk to school from the Reisinger home was a three-mile round trip.

In 1926 Ernie's father moved to Carlisle. He left the railroad to become a salesman and was often away from home, so often that he remains a shadowy figure to his children to this day. He excelled at selling things, and his success emboldened him to begin selling oil stock. Tragically, his involvement in selling stocks and shares could not have been at a worse time, because America was heading towards Black Tuesday, 29 October 1929, and the infamous Wall Street crash.

What Ernie's father did not know was that the USA, along with Great Britain and other leading industrial and financial powers, was trying to keep the world prosperous by deliberately inflating the money supply. It was done secretly, without legislative enactment or control. There was no public knowledge, nor any expression of alarm from the business community. The amount of money in circulation remained stable, but credit expanded from $45 billion in 1921 to $73 billion in 1929. Interest rates were kept artificially low and credit inflation kept growing until the end of 1928. Six months later, the economy went into steep decline and, three months after that, the market collapsed. Speculation had been utterly uninhibited. At the peak of the craze there were about a million active speculators in America. Out of a population of 120 million, almost 30 million families were actively involved in the stock market, and the Reisingers were among them.

As Paul Johnson describes it, 'On Monday, October 21, for the first time, the ticker-tape could not keep pace with the news of the falls and never caught up. In the confusion the panic intensified (the first margin calls had gone out on the Saturday before) and speculators began to realise that they might lose all their savings and even their homes. On Thursday, October 24, shares dropped vertically with no one buying. Speculators were sold out as they failed to respond to margin calls. Crowds gathered on Broad Street outside the New York Stock Exchange, and by the end of the day eleven men well known in Wall Street had committed suicide.'[1]

Ernest Reisinger's father lost all his own money in the crash, but that was not the biggest blow to him personally. A circle of friends who had trusted him and bought stock from him now discovered they had lost large sums of money. One of his closest friends even lost his farm. These events were more than he could bear. Mr Ernest G. Reisinger became a man broken in mind and body. Losing his sanity, and utterly broken in health, he had to be placed in an institution, and from that time onwards he needed to be cared for twenty-four hours a day. He never left the institution until his death thirty years later. The Reisinger family faced a most uncertain future. Ernie's mother Cordelia faced heart-rending decisions concerning the

[1] Paul Johnson, *The History of the American People*, London: Weidenfeld and Nicholson,1997, p. 613.

placement of her children. She was forced to place Ernie and John in a children's home in Carlisle. Donald went to live with his uncle John Reisinger on a farm where he also operated a saw mill. Only the baby, Grace Esther, remained at home with her mother.

Yet during these bleak months for America, and the casualties of the Wall Street crash like the Reisinger family, things were not all hopeless, nationally or personally. In New York foundations were laid for one of the most famous buildings in the world. While Ernie and John were in the orphanage, the Empire State Building was erected in a record fourteen months. It became a symbol of the remarkable resilience of American society, with its determination to overcome its crises. Cordelia Reisinger found employment doing domestic work for the owner and publisher of Carlisle's daily newspaper. The Thompsons were particularly generous to her and her children in their payment of salary and provision of clothing and shoes for the family. Before long this new job security encouraged her to rent a small apartment and bring Ernie and John out of the orphanage, so that once again they lived together as a family. At fourteen years of age, Ernie reluctantly left high school to help his mother and his younger brothers and sister survive. They moved to a second-floor apartment, and life was a daily struggle, with only two small irregular incomes.

The children were sent by their mother to Second Presbyterian Church's Sunday School, and that congregation helped them with money for rent and food. The children wore only 'hand-me-downs' for many years. Ernie's first job, a paper route, meant delivering 120 daily newspapers in an area covering four square miles, six days a week, in all weather. On Saturdays and Wednesdays he also carried groceries for customers at the local market. In the winter he shovelled snow off the sidewalks and driveways of wealthier homes. A few years later he washed dishes for a small restaurant in the evenings for $3.00 a week, plus all he could eat. During the apple season he worked on farms, picking fruit. Whatever jobs he could get he took in order to survive and provide for his siblings and beloved mother. They were invaluable years of education and character development, though not in formal schooling.

In the Second Presbyterian Church Sunday School, Ernie sat in a class of boys his own age. Their teacher was a young lawyer named Harold Irwin. Then a lecturer in Dickinson School of Law, he was for the remainder of his life a practising lawyer in Carlisle. In the early days of their attendance, Ernie and John had to return to the orphanage when Sunday School ended. One afternoon the grimness of that prospect broke Ernie's heart. Sitting in a pew in the church he wept, and it was a big clean handkerchief offered by Harold Irwin that dried his tears. Ernie never forgot that, nor that it was Harold who came to visit him when he was in hospital with suspected pneumonia. A law professor was not too busy to devote a little time to a fatherless child. Ernie wished he could have a father like him, or even that this man would *become* his father. In fact Harold Irwin seriously considered adopting young Reisinger, but for some reason decided not to do so.

What did Ernie learn in that Sunday School, where Harold Irwin had become the superintendent? He learned to recite the books of the Bible, and the Ten Commandments. Those are great lessons, but there are greater. He learned what was right and wrong, and he realized that he lacked the ability to keep those laws in a manner that pleased God. The right road to travel through life had been set before him, but Ernie learned nothing in Sunday School of the real motive for observing those Commandments – love for the Lawgiver, who had taken the curse of the broken law from us. Nor did he learn of the source of strength for travelling that righteous road – the indwelling Spirit.

The other boys in the Sunday School class were children of church members, and soon the church's policy concerning church membership became clear: that the pastor would invite teenagers to 'join the church'. He approached Ernie and suggested that he join 'Second Pres.' The minister did first visit Cordelia, and she agreed it would be nice for her first-born son to become a church member. So, quite sincerely, the decision was taken by all concerned and Ernie and other teen-agers were registered as church members.

A stranger to God and ignorant of the Lord Jesus Christ, Ernie lacked the first qualification for church membership; he knew nothing of 'gladly receiving the word' (*Acts* 2:41). Consequently he knew nothing of a growing appreciation of the apostolic teaching of the New Testament, or of the warmth and responsibilities of Christian fellowship, or of becoming a man of prayer. Church membership for him was a minor ritual performed to please the Sunday School teacher, the minister and his mother. He had no interest in sermons or services of worship, and soon he ceased attending Second Presbyterian Church. He drifted along to places where other teenagers assembled, like the YMCA, the pool hall and the bar. He was entering the adult world without knowledge of himself, the purpose of life or God's plan of salvation. In spite of this tenuous contact with church, he had become another twentieth-century pagan.

3

ELMER ALBRIGHT

IN HIS EIGHTEENTH YEAR Ernest Reisinger took his first full-time job as a trackman on the Pennsylvania Railroad. At that time he met Mima Jane Shirley, the girl who was to be his wife for more than sixty years. He soon proposed to her, and they were married on March 30 1938. Eleven months later their only child Donald was born. Before his twentieth birthday Reisinger had taken a wife and become a father.

Upon marrying his beloved Mima, he entered into a close and loving family. Her father, Russell Shirley, was a fine man, a master journeyman carpenter and a key employee in a large construction company. He helped get Ernie a job as a labourer with his company for 35 cents an hour. The following year Ernie's lifelong characteristic of energetically applying himself to any work set before him resulted in his becoming an apprentice carpenter, and before long, a journeyman. His skills and interest in the construction business also developed through his involvement in building the Pennsylvania Turnpike.

The Pennsylvania Turnpike began as an idea for a railroad – the 'South Pennsylvania Railroad'. William Vanderbilt envisioned a high-speed line going across Pennsylvania to connect the east coast with Pittsburgh and points farther west. He began construction of the line in 1883 by grading right-of-way and digging seven tunnels. Political and financial manoeuvring forced Vanderbilt to abandon this project on 1 July 1886, leaving half-finished tunnels and miles of graded right-of-way.

In the 1930s Pennsylvanians with childhood memories of playing on the right-of-way and in the tunnels, lobbied the Pennsylvania legislature to consider building an 'all-weather' highway using Vanderbilt's abandoned right-of-way. A model of this new super-highway was displayed at the General Motors *Highways and Horizons Futurama* exhibit at the 1939 New York City World's Fair. The new turnpike was envisaged as a different form of highway in America, similar to Germany's 100-mph *autobahns*.

The first stretch of the Turnpike commenced just outside Carlisle in Middlesex and ended in Irwin, east of Pittsburgh, covering a distance of one hundred and sixty miles. To construct the project on schedule in twenty months, 1,100 engineers were employed. There were over three hundred bridges to be built and, after plans were completed in October 1938, 155 construction companies and 15,000 workers from eighteen states, including this young father Ernest Reisinger, came under contract to the Turnpike Commission. His activities were modest for a twenty-year old and involved making the concrete forms for the bridges. Though the work on the Turnpike began slowly, soon fifty crews of men were laying down the road at a staggering pace of three-and-a-half miles a day. The Pennsylvanian Turnpike became the model for the whole vast network of roads that now traverses continental USA.

Working on the Pennsylvania Turnpike fed Ernie's hunger for knowledge and gave him vision and new expertise, but he had no intention of spending his life as a carpenter. Great enterprises developing around him stimulated his gifts of leadership and management. So Ernie enrolled for distance learning from the Chicago Technical College, studying Blueprint Reading, Estimating and Building Superintendence. After successfully completing these studies he joined a large construction company, Irwin and Leighton in Philadelphia. His first job was at the Aberdeen Proving Ground in Maryland, a famous government project in a vast military area containing ballistics testing grounds. The Reisingers found a brand new home in Maryland and moved there. When the first job was completed, the government awarded Ernie civil-service status, so the family decided to settle down in the area.

This should have been the happiest time in Reisinger's life, what with a beautiful wife, a healthy baby boy, the security of a job with a good living wage, and future ambitions. Yet in fact these were proving to be among his very worst days. He began to drink heavily and miss days at work. Having wormed its way into his life all those years ago, alcohol became an adversary with which Ernie would always have to do battle. Bouts of drinking caused so much stress at home that Mima was seriously considering taking their son and heading back to live with her parents. There was an enormous vacuum at the heart of Ernest Reisinger's life. Surely, he pondered, there must be more to man's brutish existence than sleeping, working and eating? He seemed to have everything, but he felt he had nothing

It was at that time that God sent a man across Reisinger's path who would change his whole way of life. Elmer Albright was a fellow carpenter, born in Shamokin, Pennsylvania, whose father was a coal miner. He and his wife Evie had come to know Jesus Christ as their Lord and Saviour at the Christian and Missionary Alliance Church in Shamokin about five years earlier under the ministry of a Scotsman named George Atcheson. As he worked with Ernie, Elmer began to speak to him of the Lord Jesus Christ, someone he invariably referred to as his Saviour. He told Ernie of God the Creator who made and sustained the universe, whose Son, the Lord Jesus Christ, had been sent into the world to deal with our greatest need, the guilt of our wayward living: 'We deserve eternal death because we are sinners, but the Lord Jesus, because he loved us, died for us.' While Elmer explained the good news to him, and urged him to read the Bible, he invited Ernie to come to the Sunday School which the government allowed a small group of Christians to hold in a recreational building on the base.

Elmer Albright and Reisinger had many conversations over the course of a year, but the other workmen had little time for Elmer. He was a good carpenter and a considerate fellow-worker, but he had this 'bug' on religion. 'Don't get too close to him,' they warned Ernie. 'If you do, all he will talk about is religion.' But the men were wrong. Elmer never talked about religion. He talked about the Lord Jesus Christ in such an intimate way that Ernie began to think, 'He really knows this Person.'

Some of the men used to make snide remarks when Elmer bowed his head over lunch to thank God for his food. They would badger him with such archaic questions as, 'Elmer, where did Cain get his wife?' Elmer would smile and say, 'Aw, I'm a Christian. I don't bother with other men's wives', and continue with his work. The men would poke fun at him, but one thing they could not deny: Elmer lived a consistently good life. He truly cared for this young man Ernie Reisinger, and so every Friday he would ask him, 'Coming to Sunday School this week?' For a year Ernie's reply was to shake his head. He had fifty-two excuses for not attending a Christian gathering, but Elmer never stopped his kindly speaking to and praying for this unhappy young man.

On Sundays Ernest Reisinger would watch children cross his yard on their way to Elmer's Sunday School. A longing grew in his heart that his son Donald should attend as he had done when he had been a little boy. Now aged four, Donald had never set a foot inside a church or had an ounce of Christian instruction. He had never heard the name of Jesus uttered except in profanity. So after refusing invitations for an entire year, one Sunday morning Ernie surprised everyone by taking Donald to Sunday School, but his chief reason was that the little boy should be acquainted with religious people who would take care of him spiritually, thereby relieving Ernie of that responsibility.

Ernest Reisinger sat there throughout the meeting, but failed to understand it. When the Sunday School class stood and sang a familiar hymn, 'What a friend we have in Jesus, All our sins and griefs to bear', he could not lift up his voice with them because those words were not true for him. 'I closed the hymnbook', he later said. When he returned home, the words of that hymn went round and round in his brain. He determined that he would not return to Sunday School. Once was more than enough, and thus a month or two passed by. Ernie grew increasingly miserable, more than ever before, even more than during his childhood stay of several months in the Carlisle orphanage. He wondered whether he were having a nervous breakdown. He knew nothing of God the Holy Spirit's work of conviction, preparing the heart of man for salvation. Reisinger was deeply troubled about his sins, and concerned about the whole tenor of his life.

Eight weeks later, albeit reluctantly, but feeling there was nowhere else for him to turn, Ernie returned with Don and Mima to the Sunday School. There was Elmer Albright waiting at the door. As Ernie stretched out his arm to shake hands with Elmer, he glanced up at his face and saw tears running down Elmer's cheeks. Ernie thought, 'How odd – what is emotional about shaking hands?' Elmer's tears made no sense to him until later when he learned of Another One who wept, and whose compassion Elmer also shared. He had refused to give up on Ernie.

Elmer believed in the power of the gospel, that Jesus Christ is Absolute Reality, that his salvation is divine, and that regeneration is a work of God that changes sinners. Elmer believed that the Lord Jesus continues to save men and women today. That faith had made him a man of prayer. Soon afterwards Ernie went to Elmer's home and met his wife Evie. She said to him, 'So, you are Ernie Reisinger? I didn't know who Ernie Reisinger was, but I was hoping that he would soon move or get converted.' All this was new language for Ernie and he looked perplexed at Evie Albright. She then explained to him that on many occasions after Elmer came home from work, before supper, he would go to his bedroom, close the door, and begin to pray. Evie would watch the dinner getting cold and then walk quietly to the door behind which her husband was crying to God for somebody named 'Ernie Reisinger'.

That second Sunday afternoon, when the Sunday School was over, Reisinger invited Elmer to come over to his house. Elmer brought along with him the superintendent of the Sunday School and a woman teacher. They happened to come from different denominations: Elmer Albright belonged to the

Christian and Missionary Alliance; the superintendent was a Methodist; the woman teacher was a Baptist. Ernie did not learn that from their conversation, but much later, for none of them asked him to join their organizations. They brought Bibles with them and talked to him about the Lord Jesus Christ. Salvation, they all agreed, had nothing to do with keeping the Ten Commandments, nor joining any particular church, nor participating in baptism or the Lord's Supper. It was to be found in the great work the Lord Jesus Christ alone had done. Man's response could only be to receive the gift of eternal life which God offered to men and women for the sake of his love for his Son.

Ernest Reisinger listened earnestly and intently, and they prayed with him before leaving and gave him some leaflets to read. That night Ernie became deeply serious about his relationship with God. If there was such a thing as salvation, he wanted it. He determined on Monday that settling this matter was more important than going to work. He stayed home and read the leaflets his friends from the Sunday School had brought him. After his wife went to bed, he brought out the family Bible, removing the four-leaf clover and the baby curls from within its cover. Then he prayed, 'Dear God, if You be . . . if You exist, let me know something about being saved.' It was the first honest prayer of his life.

Then he began to open the Bible, turning over pages at random. He found it baffling, especially the genealogies and the strange actions of the men of the Old Testament. He could not find anything about how to be saved. He turned from this page to that, Old Testament and New Testament – it was all a sealed book to him. He kept dipping into it in his frustration but gaining no insights. Then eventually he came across a little piece of paper tucked between two pages. It was a tract, and written boldly on the cover were the words, 'What Must I Do to be Saved?' The tract told him that he had sinned against God and that he would get nowhere unless he acknowledged that to him. Ernest C. Reisinger knelt down in his living room and prayed the prayer of the publican of whom Jesus spoke in the gospel, 'God be merciful to me a sinner.' The tract then directed him to John chapter 5, verse 24. There he read these words, 'Verily, verily, I say unto you, he that heareth my word, and believeth on him that sent me hath everlasting life, and shall not come into condemnation, but is passed from death into life.' As the words in all their simplicity and hope registered in his mind and affections, Ernie's heart was flooded with the assurance that Christ was now his Lord; he sat weeping before the Bible. On that day, through true repentance for his sins, and by faith in the Lord Jesus Christ, Reisinger knew he had met the God of grace.

Elmer Albright found a church with an evening service not far from the Aberdeen Proving Ground and encouraged Reisinger to come along with him. There Ernie first bore testimony to his new life in Christ. It happened to be a Salvation Army gathering and Ernie was drawn by their zeal, but perplexed by the absence of the ordinances of baptism and the Lord's Supper. Both his neighbours were Southern Baptists; in fact, one woman, the daughter of a minister, lived as consistent a life as his friend Elmer. After her husband had been killed in an accident at the Aberdeen Proving Ground, she had displayed much trust in God through those dark months. She urged Ernie to speak to her minister. He was helpful to Ernie, and soon Ernie was baptized in the First Southern Baptist Church of Havre de Grace, Maryland.

Many years later a telephone call told Ernie and Mima that Elmer Albright had passed away. Then living in Carlisle, about a hundred miles from Elmer's home, they determined to go to his funeral service. Leaving early one morning, they were the first to arrive at the funeral parlour where, in the empty room, the body of Elmer Albright lay in its coffin. Reisinger had an undisturbed time to stand there at the casket, quietly meditating and thanking God for his grace in bringing this humble, courageous man into his life, one who would not stop speaking to or praying for him. Then a steady stream of people began to trickle into the room. The funeral director had not expected so many to attend. Elmer and his wife had had no children, but there were two nephews of theirs whom they had loved as if they had been their own. Soon another row of chairs was needed, and another, and another. Then the room was full, but still people were coming in, so that eventually the funeral director had to open the partition at the back of the room and put out additional rows of chairs there too, until that room was almost full.

At the end of the service Ernest Reisinger approached one of the nephews, Jack Mangle, and inquired how many of these people attending Elmer's funeral service were known to him. The vast majority of them were strangers to Jack. So Reisinger wandered about the room and listened as people spoke to one another after the service. He was deeply impressed by the number who told others that Elmer's testimony and influence on their lives had inspired them to become Christians. There are probably men in the pulpit and on the mission field today because of the example of this modest, anonymous Christian.

4

THE NAVY

In 1943, soon after joining the Southern Baptist Church of Havre de Grace, Reisinger enlisted in the United States Navy. The Pacific War was well under way by this time. The USA had sought to stay out of the war in Europe until Japan threw in its lot with the Axis powers. On Sunday, 7 December 1941, Japanese planes attacked the American fleet moored in Pearl Harbor, Hawaii. The raid was one of the most audacious and complex schemes of its kind in military history. It involved moving a gigantic carrier force unobserved over thousands of miles of ocean, and it achieved complete tactical surprise. The Japanese planes attacked at 7.55 a.m., with a second wave following an hour later. All but twenty-nine Japanese planes returned to their carriers by 9.45 a.m., and the entire force got away without loss. The attacks destroyed half of America's military air power in the entire theatre, put eight battleships, three destroyers, and three cruisers out of action, and sank the battleships *Oklahoma* and *Arizona*. Two thousand, three hundred and twenty-three U.S. servicemen were killed.

Great was the political risk which Japan took in treacherously attacking an enormous and intensely moral nation like the United States before a formal declaration of war. When the Japanese envoys handed their message to the Secretary of State on that Sunday afternoon, he set the tone for the American response: 'In all my fifty years of public service I have never seen a document that was more crowded with infamous falsehoods and distortions on a scale so huge that I never imagined until today that any government on this planet was capable of uttering them.' Until Pearl Harbor, America had been an ineffectual observer of the Second World War. It was remote, divided, with a leadership lacking in firm purpose. After Pearl Harbor it was instantly united, angry and committed to waging total war with all its outraged strength. The following week Adolf Hitler recklessly declared war on America and so drew upon his own nation a full measure of the enormous fury spawned by Pearl Harbor.

In May of 1942 Japan suffered its first Pacific setback when an invasion force heading for New Guinea, engaged at long range by American carriers in the Coral Sea, was so badly damaged that it had to return to base. On June 3 another invasion force heading for Midway Island was outwitted and defeated, losing four of its carriers and the flower of the Japanese naval air force. Japan had already effectively lost naval air-control of the Pacific.

Meanwhile, the United States embarked on a mobilization of human, physical, and financial resources without precedent in history. All the inhibitions, frustrations, and restraints of the Depression years vanished virtually overnight. Within a single year the number of planes built in America jumped to over 48,000. It created an army with more than seven million personnel by 1943. U.S. shipyards turned out 88,000 ships and landing-craft during that same year. During the conflict, the United States enrolled 4,183,466 sailors, one of whom was a twenty-four-year-old Pennsylvanian named Ernest C. Reisinger.

At the age of sixteen, afer lying to the recruiting officer about his age, Ernie had attempted to join the Navy. The kindly man knew that Ernie was too young for military service, but turned him down on the pretence that he lacked 'a proper bite'. Eight years later, with war fever gripping America, the Navy was not so particular about the jaw alignment of its recruits. 'The officer felt the back of my head and said, "You're warm. You're in!"', said ECR. He could have deferred military service because of his civil service job at a government military installation, but Ernie was zealous to serve his country rather than stay at home. Both his younger brothers, Donald and John, had already enlisted. Ernie could not ignore their sacrifice and choose a less dangerous war for himself at the Aberdeen Proving Ground.

It was to the Bambridge Naval Base in Maryland that Reisinger was sent for basic training. At this boot camp he met a devout Pentecostal who tried unsuccessfully to get him to speak with tongues. After basic training he was assigned to the *U.S.S. Westmoreland,* an amphibious attack transport vessel commissioned at Hoboken, New Jersey. He served as a Second-Class Carpenter's Mate, a Second–Class petty officer.

On the train to Hoboken, Ernie sat beside another young sailor named George Merisotis, who was also heading for the *Westmoreland*. George had already seen action in the Atlantic but now was being transferred to this amphibious vessel. Ernie was reading his pocket New Testament and this intrigued the young sailor next to him. 'Are you reading your prayer book?' he asked. 'Yes,' said Ernie, 'there are a lot of prayers in this book.' Silent for a while, George then asked, 'Do you believe in confession?' He had been raised in the Greek Orthodox church, and one of the differences between that church and the Roman Catholic is that their adherents do not go to a confessional to list out their sins to a priest. George wanted to know where Ernie stood on this ecclesiastical issue. Ernie told him that the Bible told men to confess their sins to God. Turning to the First Epistle of John, he read to George these words, 'If we confess our sins, he is faithful and just to forgive us our sins, and to cleanse us from all unrighteousness' (*1 John* 1:9). Those words gripped George. He had probably never heard any words from the New Testament before that train ride.

Just as Elmer Albright had patiently spoken to this young carpenter, so he now had many conversations with George. 'Greek' (his nickname on the ship) was described by a friend as 'a rather husky athletic-built man with a big smile exposing pearly white teeth with open spaces between them'. Ernie explained the gospel to him and answered his questions. The two men became true friends. God blessed that friendship and through Ernie's testimony, somewhere between New Jersey and Honolulu, George turned to Jesus Christ in faith and repentance. It was an undramatic conversion. In Honolulu, Greek was actually baptized, though Ernie, sick for a few days in hospital, missed the service.

They served together throughout the war and stayed in contact until George died in 1997. There were a few other Christians on the ship and one of them, Charles Kauffman, was very impressed by meeting this new follower of Jesus Christ. Writing home, he told his friends about Greek:

'He tells anyone and everyone that Jesus saved him. We see stamped on his dog tags a large G.O. What does it mean? "Greek Orthodox". Even though I am an older Christian, his zeal and faithfulness challenge me. He can quote enough Scripture to show anyone God's way of salvation. His name is George Merisotis, but we all know him as "Greek".'

George Merisotis got through the war safely and returned home to get married. For some years all was well, but then his marriage went through a rocky period. He wrote to Reisinger recalling the wonderful times they had shared together in their prayer locker on the *Westmoreland*. Those were the days, he wrote, that he would cherish for ever. Then he apologized for some years of silence: 'I am ashamed of myself. The truth is, I had sunk into some sin and was not wanting to have anything to do with anyone. But about three weeks ago I heard Charles Fuller on the radio and he was preaching on the subject of the last days. Oh, how it stirred me! I truly asked God's forgiveness and am once more memorizing and reading God's Word.' George had kept God on the fringes of his life for more than eight years.

For a while things were better in the Merisotis home until Reisinger received a call from George informing him that his wife was threatening to leave. He pleaded with Ernie to make the long journey to his home and help him. When Ernie arrived he found that Mrs Merisotis had packed and gone. The home had tracts set down everywhere. There was hardly a surface, not even the bathroom, not covered by some gospel leaflet. Ernie and George faced one another. 'Read the opening verses of John's First Epistle', said Ernie. George found the passage and began to read, 'That which was from the beginning, which we have heard, which we have seen with our eyes . . . ' 'Stop!' said his old friend. 'Read that again.' George looked at him and read the section again: 'That which was from the beginning, which we have heard, which we have seen with our eyes . . . ' 'Stop!' said Ernie again. 'Read that again.' George looked at the words, and then more slowly began to read the opening words of the First Epistle of John: 'That which was from the beginning, which we have heard, which we have seen with our eyes . . . ' 'Stop there', said Ernie. 'What has your wife seen in you of "the Word of Life"? She has seen your tracts everywhere, but has she seen Jesus Christ in your life day by day?'

Attempts at marital reconciliation ultimately failed, and Ernie suggested to George that he come to Carlisle and join the close fellowship of Grace Baptist Church. So the last decades of George's life were spent in Carlisle. George opened a restaurant and sandwich shop which became a flourishing business. His belief in the usefulness of tracts never left him, and he set up a rack near the shop's entrance where, over the years, thousands were taken away by his customers. George Merisotis died in Carlisle in 1997. He and Ernie had been friends for fifty-three years.

* * * * *

The *U.S.S. Westmoreland* sailed through the Panama Canal and, after a few weeks of invasion manoeuvres in the Honolulu area, headed on to the South Pacific. It called at the ports of Manila Bay, Luzon, Lungalian Gulf and Okinawa. Reisinger and his fellow sailors had covered eighty thousand miles. Twice the *Westmoreland* returned to the U.S.A. to pick up Marines and re-supply the ship, only to return to the South Pacific.

Amongst the crew Reisinger discovered other Christians such as Charles Kauffman and Marvin Gilley. They met together regularly with another three or four men – Smitty, Eugene, Fred and Johnson – in Number Four Hold. Here they sang, studied the Bible and prayed, with Ernie leading and exhorting the group. Charles Kauffman introduced him to the

Navigators organization. Ernie still keeps the packs of verses he carried around with him on the ship. While standing in line for a meal, he would memorize a verse from the Bible – servicemen seemed to spend half their days waiting in line. The crew gave him the nickname 'Deacon'. He learned every verse in the Navigators' memory system, and then wrote out other important verses to memorize. Those hundreds of verses later became an invaluable support to him in counselling and preaching. In the weekly meetings in Number Four Hold, Ernie encouraged the men to learn the Scriptures. They would end their time together by kneeling and praying. After the war both Charles Kauffman and Marvin Gilley became pastors, but the first pastorate did not work out well for Charles. He too moved to Carlisle and took a job with a heating and plumbing company. Then, after regaining confidence to return to the ministry, he pastored a church in Wauseon, Ohio until his retirement in 1997. Marvin Gilley retired from his pastorate in 1992.

Not all the crew were sympathetic with this Christian witness. One man, a mean 'smart Alec', took an immense dislike to Ernie, referring to him as 'Shorty'. He wasted no opportunity for 'rubbishing' Ernie. One day the ship lost mail, much to the discouragement of the whole crew, because the greatest single boost to morale was receiving a letter from one's wife, girl-friend or parents. 'No, nothing for you, Shorty', the man snarled, adding other unsavoury comments, and brandishing the two letters that he himself had received. Then he snarled at Ernie, 'If I want you I'll throw you a bone.' That was it! Ernie threw a couple of punches and decked the man.

Below deck Reisinger had made a little space he had come to call his own. It was a hideaway in a damage-control centre into which he had cut an air-vent. There he spent hours with his Bible and Halley's *Bible Handbook*; sometimes entire days could be taken up with a study of the Scriptures. After flooring his tormentor, he knelt there and wept before God. He had sinned by retaliating instead of turning the other cheek. His witness to the ship's company was ruined. It was there that George found him, putting his arm around him and comforted him. 'I think your stock has gone up with some of the men', he said.

This same anger was displayed on another occasion as the men lined up for their evening meal. Another clown was dishing out the food into the trays held by the sailors. He would sometimes deliberately put the custard on top of the potatoes, or the dessert into the soup. Ernie watched his mischief with increasing hostility, resolving that if he were foolish enough to do that for him he would learn a swift lesson. And he did! As he poured the custard over the vegetables, Ernie shoved the whole tray of food straight into the man's leering face. Then, without his meal, he walked up to the deck and leaned dejectedly over the rail, thinking to himself again how he had spoiled his witness to the Lord Jesus. There, the Bosun's Mate found him: 'I have been waiting for days for someone to do that to that guy', he told Reisinger. But his explosive anger was something Ernie needed to mortify by the power of the Holy Spirit, and even into old age his short fuse would be a battle for him. There would come other times when he would continue to mar his witness to Christ by giving in to a fit of rage against those he loved most.

Towards the end of the war, the ship was directed to sail for Japan and prepare for invasion. This announcement led to a sharp increase in the attendance at the Christian fellowship in Number Four Hold. From about eight participants, the group increased in number to twenty or thirty. The ship's company prepared to invade Sasabo, a Japanese shipyard, but the atomic bombs dropped on Hiroshima and Nagasaki changed the defiance of Japan's leadership. Even as the ship approached the coast, Japan surrendered and both sides declared a cease fire. Not all the Japanese soldiers in Sasabo realized this and some fired at the *Westmoreland*, but no one was hit, and Ernest Reisinger's war was over. It had been a time of considerable spiritual growth for the carpenter.

5

CHANGES IN THE FAMILY

ERNEST REISINGER'S FIRST CONCERN after coming to know God for himself was that his family members also should become Christians. Initially they were the most sceptical of hearers and his early enthusiasm was quickly tempered by their indifference to his message and suspicion of his zeal. They judged him as the one in need of help, and supposed that this new excitement for religious matters would quickly end. His mother, in fact, took Mima aside and told her that unless her husband stopped reading the Bible he would lose his mind.

Donald Reisinger, his younger brother, was the first of the family to be converted. Even before Ernie had joined the Navy Don had been persuaded to accompany his brother to an evangelistic meeting. It had not been a success. The preacher was long-winded and Donald's girlfriend Bonnie (his future wife) was waiting elsewhere to meet him, so that he had only half his mind on the sermon. 'Don't talk to me about religion again', he told Ernie, who honoured that request. But he continued to pray for his brother, and the Holy Spirit began to work in Donald's life. Consequently Donald became convicted that he was a sinner in the sight of the living God. One day, far from a religious meeting, without the eloquence or pressures of any evangelist, Donald parked his car on a mountain road and, sitting there, began to read the Old Testament prophet Jeremiah. As he came across these words, 'You shall seek me and find me when you search for me with all your heart' (*Jer.* 29:13), in that mountain fastness, Donald cried out to God to have mercy upon him and found assurance that his prayers had been heard.

The fact that now two of the Reisinger brothers had become Christians changed the dynamics of family relationships. Donald too became a witness to the grace of God in Jesus Christ. He married Bonnie who also became a Christian. They joined a Presbyterian church where the gospel was faithfully preached and after some years Donald was appointed an elder in that congregation. Later they settled in Delaware and joined a Southern Baptist church in which he served as a deacon. He died in 1989. Ernie's sister, Grace, and her husband also came to faith in Christ, establishing a Christian home, and becoming active members of a Presbyterian Church. All four of their children made credible professions of faith in Christ, and the oldest son, Craig Lins, serves as a minister in a Presbyterian Church in America congregation in Delaware.

The youngest brother, John Reisinger, had gone straight from school into the war in the South Pacific, and he and Ernie never saw one another until they were discharged from the Navy. They had always talked about going into the construction business together, so they settled in Carlisle and established Reisinger Brothers Construction. John had married a nominal Roman Catholic from St Louis, Missouri, and, while in the Navy, he had attended some preparation classes to join the Roman Church himself, though nothing had come of that. His mother had written him a letter while he was in the Navy telling him, 'I think your brother Ernie has had a nervous breakdown. He goes to church every Sunday – Sunday nights too, and also every Wednesday night. He's always handing out pieces of paper to people.'

Ernie was the first man to talk to John about his sin and need of the Lord Jesus Christ, doing so at every opportunity until John became increasingly frustrated with these conversations. Had he not already been a member of two different churches? One night while he was walking home in Carlisle a stranger confronted him, 'Are you saved?' he asked him. John replied, 'No, but my brother is.'

John increasingly wanted to become a true Christian, yet, as a twenty-one-year-old heathen, he wanted to go on living the way he enjoyed. So, to escape his trouble of conscience, he decided it was time to get away from his older brother and his little black book. He went to Ernie and recommended that he buy out his half-interest in their partnership. He and his wife Rose Mary decided to move a thousand miles away to her home town of St Louis. Rose Mary feared that her husband would soon become just like Ernie who, she thought, wanted simply to work and go to church, while John and she wanted another lifestyle.

Ernest Reisinger was discouraged that the partnership had been terminated, that the message of the cross of Christ had become offensive to John, and that his kid brother had left Carlisle for St Louis. How would John come to know God now? How little of God's ways did Ernie then know. John began work in St Louis with a construction company and in his first weeks there, standing on the roof of a building, a fellow carpenter began to talk to him about Jesus Christ. 'I've only met two nuts in the world,' replied John curtly, 'my own brother and you.'

After two years of keeping God out of their lives, John and Rose Mary Reisinger decided to return to Carlisle and work for Reisinger Brothers Construction. By this time Donald had also been converted, and both he and Ernie were praying for John and witnessing to him. They would invite him to meetings, but John would lie and use every possible excuse not to attend. One evening when he dropped in at Ernie's home, he discovered that his brothers were on their way out to a meeting. 'Come with us. Come on John', they pleaded, and the next thing this reluctant brother remembers was riding in a car with them on his way to hear a preacher.

John describes what occurred that night in these words:

'When we arrived and the preaching began, I was never so angry in my life. I sat there and gritted my teeth. I looked at one brother and then at the other. "You dirty rotten so-and-so's . . . you set me up . . . you told this preacher that I was coming, and you even told him everything about me." But I had to sit there and listen, and soon God was speaking to my heart. I went home from that meeting like the blind man who met Jesus: I had been blind, but now I could see – and God had done it.

'When I got home, everyone was sitting around the table playing a game. Rose Mary looked up at me, and commented, "What's happened to you? You look as happy as a lark." "Why shouldn't I be? I got saved", I said. There was a long silence and she started to cry, saying, "You aren't going to be a religious fanatic like your brother, are you?" She didn't speak to me for about six weeks. But at some point, God began to open her heart too, and bring her to a knowledge of the truth. Within another month, she also had become a Christian.'

Within a few years John Reisinger left the construction business to study at the Lancaster Bible School in Pennsylvania, and went on to pastor a church in nearby Lewisburg. There he was befriended by an older Christian by the name of I. C. Herendeen who owned the Bible Truth Depot. Herendeen, who published and sold Christian literature, always took time to talk to John and give him books. John Reisinger made steady advances in understanding the Christian faith and shared these with his older brothers, though not without encountering many reservations and some hostility from Ernie. This was a case of role reversal.

Their mother, Cordelia Reisinger, was the last family member to become a Christian, and that occurred about fifteen years after Ernie was converted. What had happened to her sons and daughter was initially fearful to her, but she finally came to appreciate the change in all her children. Thus interest was stirred in Christianity, and Cordelia had some kind neighbours who were faithful church-attenders. It did not take much persuasion on their part for her to join them at their church. Unfortunately she became a member of a liberal and lifeless church and, once she thought she had religion, her children's difficulty in speaking to her about the Lord Jesus was considerably increased. So the years went by with her children loving her, giving her books, praying for her, and at times witnessing to her about personal reliance on the Lord Jesus as an all-sufficient Saviour.

One day Ernie received a letter from his mother telling him that she had read the Bible from cover to cover, and in this exercise she had made an important discovery, that she needed a new birth. She sought this from God, and had come to believe that God had granted this grace to her. She was now telling her son that she intended to be baptized. Thereupon she left her dead church and joined one in which the Bible was at the centre of all its life and practices.

There was joy in the homes of her four children as this news was passed from one family to another. 'Believe in the Lord Jesus and you will be saved – you and your household', as Paul had said to the Philippian jailor (*Acts* 16:31).

6

EXPANSION IN THE BUSINESS WORLD

IT WAS IN 1946 that twenty-six-year-old Ernest Reisinger and his youngest brother John, just in his early twenties, had ventured into the building trade. Their first job was converting a large hog pen into a chicken house. They did odd jobs like remodelling homes, and then they took a giant step forward when they decided to build a house. It sold immediately, and so they were encouraged to build two houses, both of which were purchased just as quickly. They then built four houses, and there was no delay in selling them.

At that point John moved to St Louis while Ernie came to believe that he needed to further his formal education if he were one day to become a preacher. Having passed his General Educational Development (GED) examinations he successfully applied for admission at Dickinson College. He took a full course for three semesters but found it impossible to continue. The construction business was booming, he had begun to preach every Sunday in Biddle Mission, Carlisle, and was also leading a prayer meeting every Wednesday night. So he gave up his studies at Dickinson and his formal education ended.

The first big job undertaken by Reisinger Brothers, Inc. (the firm incorporated in 1952) was to build a fifty-two-unit apartment block for the United States War College. Once the company successfully completed that job, the contracts began to flow in: a highway in Shippensburg Borough, a bridge and highway in Luzerne County, highways in Adams, Cumberland and Perry Counties, sanitary sewers and water treatment plants in New Oxford and in East Pennsboro Township, and one in Carlisle Borough which cost almost a million dollars in 1961, street construction in Hanover, earth dikes for the Bethlehem Steel Company in Hanover (costing almost half a million dollars), golf-course greens, earth dams, an athletic field, water lines, storm sewers, and housing off-site utilities. All these projects were successfully completed. In 1963 the company built the large Allen Junior High School in Lower Allen Township in Cumberland County at the cost of over a million and a half dollars. In 1964 it constructed the Dickinson College Student Union Building in Carlisle for almost $2,000,000. For almost the same price the Lebanon County home was completed in Lebanon, Pennsylvania, in 1965. Waynesboro Senior High School was also built, as was Central Dauphin Junior High School.

Reisinger Brothers, Inc. (by this time operated solely by Ernest Reisinger) built for such customers as the U.S. Corps of Engineers, the Navy, the Air Corps, the Army and the Department of the Interior. He constructed buildings, roads and bridges for many Pennsylvania agencies: the General State Authority, Department of Forests and Waters, Department of Highways, State Public School Building Authority, Department of Property and Supplies, Railroad Company and United Telephone Company. He completed construction work for Maryland School Boards, the Bureau of Engineering and

Construction, and Bethlehem Steel Company. Private industries, churches and colleges invited him to build for them throughout two full decades, 1946 to 1966. The company had the flexibility to take on projects small and large, simple and complex.

The staff grew to exceed one hundred and fifty employees, with hundreds of pieces of construction equipment scattered over a dozen projects in twenty-seven central Pennsylvania counties, and also in the adjoining states of Delaware, Maryland and West Virginia. From converting a hog pen into a chicken house, Reisinger Brothers had grown to become a multi-million-dollar construction company with a national reputation. All this took place under the guidance of Ernie Reisinger. The little boy who had once lived in an orphanage in Carlisle and often cried himself to sleep had risen to enjoy a position of respect and trust in the community.

As the construction work prospered far beyond his wildest dreams Reisinger took the decision to diversify, initially for tax purposes. He bought a couple of farms and went into the dairy business with Holstein cows. At first he owned nothing but milk cows, but later he bought into show cows. Donald Reisinger his son later developed this business as president of Allen Dairy Farms, Inc. Once again a Reisinger enterprise became extraordinarily successful. The specialist magazine *Holstein World* printed an article in August 1999 summarizing the peaks in the dairy business in the USA during the last century. This is what they put on record:

'The most dominant show herd ever in Pennsylvania was that of the Allen Dairy Farms, Inc. An important nucleus of the herd was Wayne Locke's Lockway herd which was purchased in 1964. Wayne was a consultant for Allen Dairy for several years following. One of the greatest cows from Locke was Lockway Elva Lucifer (3E-96), a many-time Grand Champion with a beautiful udder. Another Lockway cow was the dam of the twice All-American Allendairy Eula Marquis (EX-92).

Allen Dairy Farms was owned by Ernie Reisinger, a successful contractor. His high-powered farm crew included Mel Hertzler, manager, Jake Emig, showman and the invaluable Ron Heffner. Don Reisinger got hooked on showing and was later president of the farm. Their years of success on the tanbark led to a roomful of trophies. One day Horace Backus was admiring the trophies and congratulated Ernie. He replied, "One of these days we're going to get a check returned stamped 'insufficient trophies'."

At the time of the Allen Dairy Sale of Champions in 1973 five All-Americans, either as individuals or as members of a produce, sold at an average of $35,800. This was the first Holstein sale in North America to have eight head bring $20,000 or more. The entire offering of 258 head averaged $2247. Maybe trophies are worth something more.

Md-Maple Lawn Marquis Glamour (EX-92), the All-American 4-Year-Old of 1971, topped the sale at $74,000, second highest price ever, at the time, for a Holstein female in North America. She was purchased by Leadfield Associates with London's Dairy Farm contender. Little did anyone know that the heifer calf she was carrying by Ivanhoe would become Allendairy Glamorous Ivy (2E-96-GMD), top of the Pearmont Dispersal in 1982 at over a million dollars.

London's Dairy was the largest buyer, taking eight head for a $141,200 total. Their purchases included the All-American Produce of 1971 and Allendairy Eula Marquis (EX-92), Allen Dairy's first All American. Jake Emig and Eula were 'joined at the hip' and he was at the halter on all her many triumphs. The produce totaled $64,000 and Eula Marquis brought $62,000.

In 1969 I was traveling with M. B. Nichols who was selecting for the National Convention Sale. Of course a stop at Allen Dairy was a must. Eula Marquis had just had her first calf, a son by Citation R. He combined three of my favorite bulls, Citation R, Marquis and Ivanhoe so I bought him and brought him to Sandy Creek. He was Allendairy Martation (VG-87) and, with the help of Ted Krueger, I got him into the Curtiss line-up. Some of my Illinois "friends" later renamed him "Mortician".'[1]

All this success came to Ernest Reisinger slowly and with much effort. His religious life was his most trusted anchor, his mainstay and comfort in his business life, as it evidently was at home and church and in his personal life. Nothing substituted for that deep-felt reliance upon God for daily help and sustenance. Equipped with the Word of God, he always had a light to guide him and the kind, loving hand of the Lord to hold him. In his darkest hours the strength of Christ inspired and consoled him. He was never alone in his entire time in the construction business. God was with him.

It is often said that a man has to be ruthless to succeed in the business world, but that was never the case with our subject. John Hurley was a churchgoer who ran a small construction company in Carlisle. There were some jobs for which he bid competitively against Reisinger Brothers, Inc. He says, 'This never interfered with our friendship and respect for one another. Ernie's company did excavation jobs that my

[1] *Holstein World*, August 1999, pp. 65 ff.

company could not do, and he did a few excavation jobs for us, including some favours that I was never able to return. On one occasion, his people gave us a price for some paving work for which we issued a contract. He discovered, after we had paid for the contract, that the price given us was higher than they normally charged. He called me about it and followed up by sending us a check. On another occasion my company bid and got a contract from the Borough. It turned out that we did not have the experience or the proper equipment to do the job economically. Ernie bailed us out and did the job for bid price even though it was pretty low. I'm sure it was not very lucrative for them and could have resulted in a loss.'

Before long John Hurley and his family resigned their membership in a liberal church to join Grace Baptist Church. He said, 'It was like being home at last, after spending half our lives in a wilderness.'

But true piety alone will never equip a man to excel in the business world. There, insight and intelligence has to be translated into competence and professionalism, so that the completed job can bear the scrutiny of the world. Without that the religion of the builder will ring hollow. One can hardly imagine how many decisions, projections and crucial situations entrepreneurs such as Reisinger face daily. The honed insights that the more privileged seek from Harvard Business School he learned in Carlisle, not even in Dickinson College, but in the school of daily experience.

The craftsmanship and reliability of Ernie's employees, the solid financial condition of the company, its practical and efficient cost control, and its track record in completing projects small and great to the satisfaction of its customers were an indispensable part of his Christian testimony. When people knew that the word of Reisinger Brothers, Inc. was good, then the firm received credit for that over a long period. People want to deal with a company that they can trust, that will stand by its commitments.

To build businesses like this there also had to be a measure of tenacity, or to use a less attractive word, toughness – the ability to fight through difficult times. The years 1946 to 1966 were not characterized by the same anti-business environment as was faced at the end of the twentieth century, but there would have been little progress if Reisinger had not been given a sanctified strength of will. Later in life, in some of his theological and ecclesiastical strivings, that same grace was to sustain him.

Yet technical knowledge alone would not have seen Reisinger Brothers, Inc. develop in the particular way it did. Though Ernest, when he began his business, had no personal knowledge of Dr Cornelius Van Til of Westminster Seminary and his teaching, he had learned, by his acquaintance with biblical theology, a kind of Christian philosophical understanding of the place business occupied in the Western world. He also had a keen appreciation of personal relationships. He sought to build trust with his employees. The old style of management – 'command and control' – is scarcely derived from the New Testament. Someone sits at the top of the pyramid and gives orders to all the others, who scurry around to carry them out. Ernie believed that the Bible calls for servant leadership, where an employer tries to make it easier for his people to do their jobs well. 'Stop in my office anytime (company time) to talk about issues', he wrote to his men, and everyone knew that he meant it and many took advantage of his offer.

Reisinger delegated responsibility and decision-making authority. He sought to respect and trust his employees, and in turn they respected him. It is not easy for an employer to deal with trade unions, and Ernie was no exception, but he believed that money and wages were not the cause of most industrial disputes. Though a generous employer himself, he felt that how one treated workmen was more important than what one paid them. One of the slogans he quoted was, 'I am looking for a dollar's worth of work for a dollar's worth of pay', but if the men were treated with respect they were a lot happier. How can any employee be comfortable if his boss pressurizes him into deceit or theft? The men who worked for Reisinger responded very favourably to his conviction that they were all in this for the long haul. They knew he wanted them to be the right team, in the right community of labour, and to do the right things. He honoured his men, as Andrew Carnegie, the great steel industrialist and benefactor had done. Carnegie once said, 'Take away my blast furnaces, take away my money, but give me my men and I will be back.' So if Ernest was asked to name the prime factor behind the success of Reisinger Brothers, Inc., he would say that on the human side it was his men, 'Give me my men.'

Three biblical principles proved to be helpful to Ernie in making those difficult day-to-day decisions which every manager faces:

1. Everything is not black and white to creatures who do not have perfect knowledge or perfect wisdom. There is only One who is omniscient. To him everything may be black or white but not to us, and may the Lord have mercy on the Christian businessman who tries to make only black and white decisions.

2. Some things are black and white such as the Ten Commandments, which are a perfect standard of right and wrong: with these there is no compromise. However, even here there

must be some merciful administration in the application of this perfect standard of righteousness.

3. Seek diligently to know the difference between compromise and the legitimate biblical principle of accommodation. That is not easy. Sometimes it is a razor-sharp line. Pray for that wisdom from above: 'But the wisdom that is from above is first pure, then peaceable, gentle, willing to yield, full of mercy and good fruits, without partiality, and without hypocrisy' (*James* 3:17).

To practise these three principles requires prudent judgment, wise and careful thinking, a gracious demeanour and a tenacious commitment to the morality summarized in the Ten Commandments; and above all it takes wisdom. 'I can truthfully say that in the twenty years in the construction business I prayed more for wisdom than anything else. I read a chapter of the book of Proverbs every day, and that took me through that book each month', Ernie Reisinger says.

The wisdom he gained could be seen in one example of a merciful application of the law of God and yet a commitment to righteousness. Reisinger Brothers, Inc. had a storage yard and warehouse, and when a man who lived in a neighbouring house saw a couple of people acting suspiciously, he believed they were looking over the contents of the yard in order to return that evening to steal selected items. He reported his suspicions to Reisinger. On another day he saw the same men looking around the storage area, and again he called the boss, warning him that that night things might be taken. Ernie got in touch with the Carlisle police and together they set up an operation to waylay these criminals. He obtained his own two-way radio for the police and waited that evening in the darkness until the thieves' vehicle drove in and the men went into the property. Ernie radioed the police who arrived in minutes and the two expected visitors were arrested and locked in a cell.

The next morning the police called Reisinger and asked him if he wanted to press charges. He told them that he wanted to talk to the men first, and so he picked up his closest friend Duke Irwin, a lawyer, and they both visited the men. 'I will not press charges,' he told the thieves, 'just as long as you attend Sunday School for a year. Also I have a job to offer both of you.' The next Sunday at 9.30 a.m. they were both in Sunday School, but after four weeks one of the men, called McKinney, ceased attending and disappeared. The other man, Wilbert Bitner, kept coming to church throughout the year, during which time he professed faith in Christ. His wife, who had had a Christian background and had watched her husband going astray, was restored to Christ. They both became active members of the Grace Baptist Church, Carlisle. He became a tireless worker as a steel rigger and because of Ernie's kindness his entire home life took on a new direction. The righteous Ernie Reisinger who loved God's law could be a compassionate man.

Ernie could also be very straight with men and women. He would explain to people his unhappiness with a profanity they used in his presence. Once he received a postcard of apology from a man to whom he had spoken about his blasphemies. Ernie replied to him thus:

March 23, 1956

Mr E., Harrisburg, Pa.

Dear Mr E.,

Thanks for your card concerning the use of the Lord's name, and I feel that I should explain my position about profanity. First, I do not deserve any apologies because taking the Lord's name in vain does not hurt me since I am only a sinner like you. However, this should convince you of one thing and that is what the Bible says about man being at enmity with God, that this is proved by our blaspheming his name . . . I say the fact that you use profanity could prove to be a blessing, for most men stay away from the Savior because they do not recognize their need. Once a man is convinced that he is a sinner, that he is at enmity with God and that actually he hates God by his very action and life – when these things become real the next step will be obvious, and that is he will flee to the Savior for the forgiveness of sin and the hope of eternal life.

I want you to understand that I am just a rotten old drunken sinner who has fled to the cross of Christ with all my sin and shame and cried out for mercy. I am thankful that there I found forgiveness and mercy for my never-dying soul. Enclosed is a little copy of part of my testimony, 'I've Found a Sure Thing', also a businessman's message to the members of his staff which I am sure you will enjoy.

I would be happy to talk with you about these things further sometime and I do appreciate your thoughtfulness in sending me the little card. As I said before it was unnecessary to apologize to me since I am a sinner like you.

Sincerely yours,

Ernest C. Reisinger

His evangelical warmth of character was displayed in a number of ways. Every day's work began with an optional prayer meeting in a room near his own office. About half-a-dozen employees of every religious denomination regularly met there and prayed together for the business, for fellow employees and their own shared needs. In addition an annual banquet took place which was first held in the year 1946. It was one of the ways in which Ernie honoured his men and their wives, and about two hundred of them came to attend each year. He would give them a word of welcome; there would be prayer before the meal; later a chairman would say a few words introducing a soloist and the main speaker. John Reisinger was a popular choice for the latter rôle in the early years. Ernie would then deliver the closing remarks. In inviting them to the banquet, he would write them an annual letter challenging them about their own relationship with God and urging them to follow Jesus Christ.

One other area of Christian service Ernie believed to be very important was his involvement in the Christian Business Men's Committee. This organization started in 1930 when several men from various business and church backgrounds desired to reach their fellow businessmen more effectively with the gospel. The arrangement they settled upon was a regular meeting of mutual encouragement with a meal and a speaker. Many of CBMC's founders were Plymouth Brethren. By 1938 an international organization had been set up, and by the end of the century CBMC has grown to about a thousand local chapters world-wide.

In 1957 Ernie took on the responsibility of organizing a CBMC committee in Carlisle. He became the chairman of the local group of men which had forty-one members in 1959. At CBMC meetings across the U.S.A. Ernest Reisinger spoke frequently. He loved this work because it encouraged Christian men to live a credible religious life and provided a natural place to invite the men he dealt with professionally to hear the gospel.

Ernie created opportunities to spread the word of Jesus Christ. He was an indefatigable witness to his Lord, both personally, in his distribution of literature and also in the letters he would write to fellow businessmen. The following letter typifies his direct kindly manner:-

May 12, 1958

Mr C., Harrisburg, Pa.

Dear Friend C.,

You keep popping up in my mind quite often and I'll be very honest with you and tell you why you do. I think of my great responsibility to those I come in contact with to entreat them to consider their relationship with Jesus Christ my Lord. I particularly think of you because it would seem that you have not considered the next world. As one of your customers I hope you won't mind me sending you a little pamphlet now and then.

Have you seen our golfing friend lately? He's quite a boy and he thinks you're great. He and I have gotten several laughs about your comment on the man who froze to death in that suit last summer. Several times we have really had a roaring laugh on that statement.

Hope you will take time to read the enclosed pamphlets. I send them with sincere interest in your soul.

Sincerely yours,

Ernest C. Reisinger

Amongst the men to whom Reisinger spoke in this way was Bill Hooke. They talked together for ten years before Bill professed faith in Christ, and subsequently he lived a changed life until the very end. Ernie showed him many Scriptures, but the one that finally struck home to his heart was the word of the Lord Jesus to Nicodemus, 'I tell you the truth, unless a man is born again, he cannot see the kingdom of God.'

In business, as in evangelism, Ernie avoided the temptation to take short-cuts. He was patient, prayerful and willing to do the right thing. It proved to be the best and only path to tread in every area. It is the way of the servant-leader. It is also the path of wisdom, involving the ability to see things in long-range perspective while taking good care of things immediately at hand. Such is an indispensable mark of a Christian businessman.

7

THE ORIGINS OF GRACE BAPTIST CHURCH, CARLISLE

NATURALLY, ON HIS RETURN TO CARLISLE at the end of the war, Ernest Reisinger went back to the Second Presbyterian Church whose Sunday School he had attended, and which had shown such kindness to his family when his father had become sick. So he, Mima and six-year-old Donald began to worship there. They soon learned about the church's links with a mission, called the Letort Mission, or Biddle Chapel, on East North Street, Carlisle. This Mission existed under the oversight of Second Presbyterian Church and its activities were run by a godly lady recognized as its deaconess. Reisinger expressed his willingness to work in the Biddle Mission and the lady, who never preached at the Mission, welcomed his support without any reservations.

At Biddle Chapel there were no week-night meetings, nor was there a Sunday evening service. The morning service was generally conducted by various men from the YMCA. Soon Ernie Reisinger was preaching there most Sundays. He organized a Sunday School class for former servicemen and also led a Wednesday-evening Bible study and prayer meeting. In addition he led the group through two Moody Bible Institute correspondence courses. These services helped a number of people and there was steady growth in the numbers attending. This was noticed by the leadership of Second Presbyterian Church and the Carlisle Presbytery commissioned him in January 1946 as a 'lay preacher'. This gave him the denomination's authority for his preaching at the Mission but it did not permit him to administer the sacraments. When the presbytery questioned him about baptism he answered that he had not yet settled on his own position. 'Will you ever preach against infant baptism?' they asked. Ernie told them that he would never preach against any issue on which his own convictions were unclear.

Daily newspapers in Harrisburg and even Philadelphia reported Ernest C. Reisinger's commissioning as a lay preacher, and pointed out to their readers that this was 'probably the first such action taken anywhere in the denomination since the commissioning of laymen was authorized last May [1945] by the General Assembly'. That 1945 General Assembly saw the ninth anniversary of the Syracuse General Assembly of the PCUSA which upheld the presbytery decision finding Dr J. Gresham Machen of Westminster Seminary, Philadelphia, guilty of defying a decision of the Assembly. It confirmed that presbytery's action of suspending Dr Machen from the ministry of the PCUSA. That reprehensible action had made the formation of the Orthodox Presbyterian Church inevitable.

The church tensions on that wider front soon came to expression in Carlisle. By the year 1950 it was becoming increasingly difficult for Ernie to continue to preach and teach freely at Biddle. Problems rose to the surface when the minister of Second Presbyterian Church expressed his unhappiness with Reisinger's teaching and evangelism, the literature he used and the guest speakers he invited to the Mission's meetings. The lay preacher was told to use solely the denominational literature of the PCUSA, and ask Presbyterian speakers exclusively to minister there. Ernie was at a crossroads. The work of the Mission had grown, and people were making professions of faith in Christ. There was a desire to practise biblical Christianity and apply New Testament church life in worship and witness, but these aims were hindered by the leadership of Second Presbyterian Church. Biddle Chapel itself was not constituted as a church. It had no membership. If anyone applied to join they were actually taken into the membership of the Second Presbyterian Church.

That was an impossible situation for Ernie to accept. He took the decision to leave the Mission, and the nucleus of believers which he had built up had to face a similar choice of bidding farewell to a place which had such happy associations for them all. Should they join a local church where they would hear the Bible taught and be encouraged in living a God-pleasing life? Reisinger had no wish to see another church started in Carlisle, so thirteen people left Biddle and began to attend the Full Gospel Tabernacle in Carlisle, an independent evangelical work. Soon they were made aware that they did not fit into that church's life. The pastor held a secular job and was happy to do so, refusing to consider leaving it to minister the Word of God in a full-time capacity. The paucity of his preparation time was evident in the thin fare of his sermons. He turned a blind eye to this influx of keen Christian people with their expectations and hunger. He himself did not have a strong gift for preaching, but he was prepared neither to step aside occasionally for others to share the work of preaching, nor to take up the full-time work of the pastorate. So that church's ministry was at a standstill and every attempt to reform it was blocked.

At the end of six months, on 5 December 1951, a small group met in an apartment and held a prayer meeting in which they also discussed the possibility of beginning a new church. Would God have them do this? There were but a few wage-earners in their midst, most of them being college and law students. Yet they experienced a unanimity that night that they should make a new start the very next Sunday, and Ernie was persuaded by their convictions. So the first assembly of Grace Chapel took place on 9 December 1951, with twenty-three people present at the Carlisle High School Band Hall in East South Street.

It was never Ernie's intention to become the pastor of this new church, and within two months, by the February of 1952, Jack Peters, a graduate of Bob Jones University, had become the first pastor. He stayed less than six months before leaving for further study, and a few months later Robert Depp accepted the call to become the minister. He remained in Carlisle for four years. During these first months the men of Grace Chapel began constructing a new building on North and Orange Street. It opened on 7 December 1952, almost exactly a year after their decision to start a new church.

Some of the new church's neighbours on North and Orange Street were not exactly overjoyed at the possibility of a church building being erected on their block. They petitioned the city to deny the congregation's request for a building to go ahead. Not for the first time did Ernie seek the help of the man who many years earlier had dried his tears with his own handkerchief at the end of a Sunday School, and come to visit him in the hospital when as a small boy he had been taken ill. Harold Irwin, now a Carlisle attorney, mediated this dispute between the new church and the neighbours to a satisfying outcome. Their concerns were laid to rest and the congregation were granted permission to locate their building on that site.

Ernest Reisinger owed an enormous debt to Harold Irwin because of his legal representation of Reisinger Brothers, Inc. Dealings with Army lawyers, insurance and Federal Housing Administration lawyers, required reams of agreements and paperwork. The accuracy, lucidity and thoroughness of the documents of this small-town lawyer surprised those men. Ernie always had a fear of letting Harold Irwin down – the man who once had been interested in adopting him as his own son. Everyone respected Irwin's integrity, and the old lawyer's commitment to Ernie's work gave weight to the contracts which were drawn up and accepted. The older man's evident trust, encouragement and affection caused Ernie no small amount of anxiety. He never wanted to let down his old friend.

In 1951 Harold Irwin approached Ernie with a query whether there was any vacancy for summer employment for his sons with Reisinger Brothers, Inc. There was, and in due course Harold Irwin, Jr. (Duke) reported for work. Married with a baby boy, Duke was a great talker and not too interested in the construction business. He had heard that Ernie was 'very religious' and was anxious to try him out. He had not been long at Reisinger Brothers, Inc. before he said to Ernie, 'If you studied Charles Darwin, he'd soon knock out your religion.' Duke had left the Presbyterian Church when he married Katie and they attended an Episcopalian Church. Ernie gave him a book entitled, *A Lawyer Examines the Bible* and Paley's *Evidences*. Little was spoken about religion for six months until one day when Duke came into Ernie's office and handed back the books. He said, 'I didn't have time to read them, and Katie is tired of dusting them.'

Next summer Duke returned for more work at Reisinger Brothers, Inc., and this time Ernie was prepared for his arrival, having regretted his failure to engage with him concerning the Christian faith the previous year. He paid Duke $50.00 a week to study some books and do research into Christianity on his behalf, the pretext being Ernie's increasing business speaking at CBMC functions. One day Ernie went into Duke's office to see the young man reading the Bible of his own volition. Before too long he was telling his mother-in-law of his assurance that he had become a Christian.

Initially Katie, his wife, resisted the message of the gospel with the utmost determination. She said in exasperation of Ernie, 'That man goes about Carlisle in a pickup truck wearing a porkpie hat and talking to everyone about being "saved". He even subscribed to Christian magazines for all the lawyers in Carlisle. I hid ours in the garbage.' Ernie longed that this young couple would both become true Christians. There was an occasion when he invited Duke and Katie to a Bible Conference at Sandy Cove, Maryland, at his own expense. Eventually Katie began to read the Bible, initially to discover all of the contradictions that she was sure it contained. Katie wanted to prove what a stupid person Ernie was.

Increasingly exasperated, she would call him with questions at all hours of the night. For example, there was one occasion when at 1.30 a.m. she phoned Ernie and grumbled passionately to him, 'It's selfish to want to be saved.' Ernie, suddenly awakened out of deep sleep by the phone ringing, could only say to her, 'Do you brush your teeth? Is that selfish?' Before long, in that summer of 1951, Katie had joined Duke in trusting in the Lord Jesus Christ.

Roger B. Irwin, Duke's younger brother, had met the Reisinger brothers over the years at the games of a church softball league. The Reisingers were both excellent fast pitchers, and several times Roger had played against them. Roger's first job in the vacation work was as a mud-mixer and hod-carrier for the bricklayers and masons who were constructing an apartment building. Many times during that first summer Ernie talked with Roger about his relationship with God and his need of Jesus Christ. Roger assured him that he had been baptized and confirmed, and that since the age of twelve he had been a member of Second Presbyterian Church.

Not content with those answers Ernie inquired about his experience of the new birth. Roger Irwin was quite assured that at heart he was 'a really nice guy'. But as Ernie continued to speak to him in the spring and summer of 1951 he became increasingly convicted of his sinful condition. One day they were walking along a street in Philadelphia and stopped in front of the window of a Christian Science Reading Room in which a pulpit Bible had been placed. The chapter before them was John 3, and it related the conversation of Jesus with 'a really nice guy' called Nicodemus, and the words were very plain, 'Jesus answered and said unto him, Verily, verily, I say unto thee, Except a man be born again, he cannot see the kingdom of God' (*John* 3:3). But it was verse 18, Roger said, that 'grabbed my attention, and I trusted Christ as my Lord and Saviour that day in early June': 'He that believeth on him is not condemned: but he that believeth not is condemned already, because he hath not believed in the name of the only begotten Son of God' (*John* 3:18). Roger saw that there was no other way but Christ. The Irwin brothers were present at the

5 December 1951 meeting when it was decided to commence a new church in Carlisle. Both the brothers became lawyers in their father's law firm and elders in Grace Baptist Church. Duke and Roger's sister, Carol, also came to faith in Christ and later married Wayne Mack, now well-known in Christian counselling circles. It has been said about Ernie's witnessing that it is just you and he in the boat, and you know to whom he is talking. Always a part of that witnessing involved literature – a book or a tract or a pamphlet that spoke to the issue at hand.

In the middle of the twentieth century, Carlisle, Pennsylvania, with its population of about fifteen thousand people was typical of northern rural and small-town America. The ministers of its mainline denominations had fallen into the arms of liberal theology, but then during the fifties there emerged among some in their congregations a concern for a better, more biblical way. Those who spoke out and confessed their faith in the Lord Jesus Christ discovered one another through that means. Drawn together whenever a prominent evangelical preacher visited a community they would express to one another the conviction that this was the sort of preaching that was needed every Sunday and not just on these rare occasions. They also listened to the same radio preachers who were all conservative men. They wanted the old doctrines of Protestantism taught again, though they were not biblically-minded enough to define what those doctrines were.

As Reisinger was a businessman, his activities touched people of every kind of religious background, more so than any of the preachers of the town who dealt largely with people of their own denominations. Walter J. Chantry, who was later to become his pastor, has written this of him:

'Reisinger was gifted by the Lord with a combination of

outstanding zeal for the Lord and winsome ways. He was skilled at communicating to others both his love for the Lord Jesus and his deep concern for the lost. Perhaps it was his own experience of being in a "far distant country", away from the Lord, which provoked his unique degree of compassion . . . Many were touched with this evident desire to bring people (especially men) to Christ and strengthen them in the faith after conversion. Thus, when others had prevailed on Ernest Reisinger to join them in founding a church that would be loyal to the Word of God, he brought not only himself, his wife Mima and his son, Don, to this group, but he had young men and women to bring along whom God had been pleased to convert under his witnessing.

'Ernie was a natural leader of this infant assembly which came to be known in 1951 as Grace Chapel (later, Grace Baptist Church). The spiritual energy of this fledgling group of young Christians was exciting. There was warm-hearted discipline in prayer, Bible study and evangelism. There was a deep hunger to learn the truth and to live a holy life. There was intense outreach into the community and a commitment to supporting foreign missions from their earliest days. Almost all of the members of the new congregation looked to Ernie as a spiritual father and leader. It was he who could focus their vision and translate it into practical steps of implementation. Perhaps the most notable features of those early years were Ernie's absorption in the things of God and his economy of time. While directing his growing business he served as a leader in a young church. While setting an example of commitment to the church he continued to serve the Lord through his ongoing efforts in personal evangelism and through extensive work for the Christian Business Men's Committee.'

8

NEW DISCOVERIES IN GRACE

DURING THE TIME JOHN REISINGER WAS STUDYING at Lancaster Bible College, Pennsylvania, he came to believe that the Bible teaches that God takes the initiative in man's salvation and that he chooses a vast number of sinners, as innumerable as the sand of the sea, to become his people. God enters into a covenant of grace to deliver these people out of their state of sin and misery and bring them into a state of salvation by a Redeemer. In other words, before creation God elected these multitudes to be saved, not on account of anything foreseen in them, but only because of his good pleasure.

John eventually had to accept that the electing grace of God was true because he met verse after verse in the Bible which said as much: 'When the Gentiles heard this, they were glad and glorified the word of God: and as many as were ordained to eternal life believed' (*Acts* 13:48); 'We know that in everything God works for good with those who love him, who are called according to his purpose. For those whom he foreknew he also predestined to be conformed to the image of his Son, in order that he might be the first-born among many brethren. And those whom he predestined he also called; and those whom he called he also justified; and those whom he justified he also glorified' (*Rom.* 8:28–30); 'Though they were not yet born and had done nothing either good or bad, in order that God's purpose of election might continue, not because of works but because of his call, she was told, "The elder will serve the younger." As it is written, "Jacob I loved, but Esau I hated"' (*Rom.* 9:11–13). 'He chose us in him before the foundation of the world, that we should be holy and blameless before him. He destined us in love to be his sons through Jesus Christ, according to the purpose of his will, to the praise of his glorious grace' (*Eph.* 1:4–6). 'We who first hoped in Christ have been destined and appointed to live for the praise of his glory' (*Eph.* 1:12). 'For we know, brethren beloved by God, that he has chosen you' (*1 Thess.* 1:4). 'We are bound to give thanks to God always for you, brethren beloved by the Lord, because God chose you from the beginning to be saved, through sanctification by the Spirit and belief in the truth' (*2 Thess.* 2:13).

Once these truths grip a man they seem to crop up everywhere in the Bible, permeating the Scriptures, and shaping his praise to God. The favourite hymn of many Christians, 'When this passing world is done', was written by Robert Murray M'Cheyne. Its theme is the vastness of our debt to the grace of God. The last stanza especially emphasizes the fact that God's choice of sinners was not based on any foreseen merit in us:

Chosen not for good in me,
Wakened up from wrath to flee,
Hidden in the Saviour's side.
By the Spirit sanctified,
  Teach me, Lord, on earth to show,
  By my love, how much I owe.

Then as one goes on to study the history of the Christian church and its great heroes one makes a further discovery, that so many men whose spirit and writings one has invariably found helpful and even inspiring, are also amongst those who believe this truth – John Bunyan, Samuel Rutherford, George Whitefield, Jonathan Edwards, David Brainerd, Adoniram Judson, William Carey, Charles Haddon Spurgeon, James Pettigru Boyce, J. C. Ryle, J. Gresham Machen, Martyn Lloyd-Jones, Donald Grey Barnhouse, Francis Schaeffer, James Montgomery Boice, Carl Henry, J. I. Packer. This list could be lengthened considerably.

But it was not through the writings of these great men, nor through his professors at the Lancaster Bible College, that John Reisinger came to believe that Christianity teaches that God chooses some sinners to be saved. He saw the truth through the words of a farmer in a small country church in Lancaster County. John puts it in his own words:

'This man was in charge of the Wednesday evening Bible study and was going through the Gospel of John. The following verses were being discussed that particular evening: "Then came the Jews round about him, and said unto him, How long dost thou make us to doubt? If thou be the Christ, tell us plainly. Jesus answered them, I told you, and ye believed not; the works that I do in my Father's name, they bear witness of me. But ye believe not, because ye are not my sheep, as I said unto you, My sheep hear my voice, and I know them, and they follow me" (*John* 10:24–27).

'The teacher had two pieces of poster board which he set on two chairs. On one poster board was written the words, HEARD AND BELIEVED, and on the other was written, WOULD NOT HEAR AND BELIEVE. The two chairs, thus labeled, represented the two groups of people spoken of in the verses being studied. Three questions were asked and each one was answered by the words of Christ addressed to the Jews. The questions dealt with the reason why some heard and believed, and why the others would not hear and believe. What made the real difference between the two groups?

'First question: "Why did the first group refuse to hear and believe the gospel?" The Saviour's words in verse twenty-six were unmistakably clear: "Ye believe not because ye are not my sheep." It was impossible to argue about the meaning of such a concise statement. Why did they not believe? Christ gave the answer, "Because you are not sheep." In other words, if they had been sheep, they would have heard and believed. The fact that they would not proved that they were not sheep. Our Lord had earlier taught the same truth. In fact his words in verse twenty-five, "I told you, and ye believed not", probably refer to the eighth chapter of John: "Jesus said unto them, If ye were Abraham's children, ye would do the works of Abraham . . . ye do the deeds of your father . . . if God were your Father, ye would love me; for I proceeded forth and came from God; . . . Why do ye not understand my speech? Even because ye cannot hear my word" (*John* 8:39–43). These people not only did not hear, but Christ said they *could not* hear. Why? They were not 'of the Father.' They were not 'Abraham's seed'. They were not among his sheep. It does not mean that they wanted to believe but Christ would not allow them to do so. Not at all, it means they were totally unable to believe because of their depravity, and God had chosen to leave them in this state. Our teacher reminded us that we all, without exception, were born with that same nature and into that same state of sin and unbelief.

'Second question: "Why did the second group hear and believe?" This question logically followed from the first one, and again the Saviour's word gave a clear answer. Verse twenty-seven said, "My sheep hear my voice". The teacher kept contrasting the two cards representing the two groups. "The gospel came to all of them, but one group believed and the other group would not. Why? What made the difference? Why did the group called 'my sheep' hear and believe? Did they have better hearts? Stronger wills? Keener minds? No, they heard because they were sheep."

'About this time the farmer turned the poster boards over. On the back of the 'HEARD AND BELIEVED' board was printed SHEEP, and on the back of the 'WOULD NOT HEAR AND BELIEVE' board was printed GOAT. Now I have always known the Bible divided men up into sheep and goats. I also knew that the sheep were God's people and the goats were not. However, I never knew until that night why some were sheep and others were not, and more specifically why I was a sheep and not a goat. It was always clear, as the cards showed, that SHEEP and HEARD AND BELIEVED belonged together, and likewise that GOAT and WOULD NOT HEAR AND BELIEVE went together. However, no one had ever shown me which was the cause and which was the effect. I had thought, as my Arminian teachers had carefully taught me, that I had decided to change my goat nature by an act of my "free will". The farmer's third question opened up the whole truth of God's sovereignty in election and forever silenced the nonsense of free will as the decisive factor in my "hearing and believing".

'The Third Question: According to our Lord's words in verses twenty-six and twenty-seven, does hearing and believing make you a sheep, or do you hear and believe because you have been chosen to be a sheep? In an instant God assured my heart of the answer. I knew which was the cause and which was the effect. The words of Christ were as clear as crystal. The Spirit of God assured me that I had heard the Shepherd's voice only because I had previously been chosen to be one of his sheep. I had willingly come to Christ only because I belonged to Christ by his sovereign election and he was claiming, by his power, in time, what had been given to him in eternity. I was not a goat that had become a sheep by a "decision of my will", but rather I was a lost sheep that had been found, and I had been found only because I was a sheep chosen from eternity. A "lost" sheep had become a "found" sheep. A goat had not become a sheep.

'Christ did not become my Shepherd when he saved me. He sought and found me only because the Father, in eternity, had given me to him to be one of his sheep. That word, "because" in verse 26 forever settled the reason some people reject the gospel. "My people hear" in verse 27 could only mean that I had heard and believed because I was a sheep from eternity. The texts can mean nothing else.

'My mind was flooded with this amazing truth: I was one of God's elect in eternity. Why had I heard and believed the gospel? Only because I had been chosen in Christ before the foundation of the world. I was not redeemed because I had believed, but rather the One who had redeemed me before I was born had now found me and revealed himself to me. Christ had sought me because I was his property. I did not become his sheep when he found me, but he had sought me and found me because I was one of his lost sheep.

'As I left that little church in Lancaster County, I looked up into the heavens with tears in my eyes. I knew that before a single star had ever shown a beam of light, God had sovereignly chosen me as a sheep and purposed to draw me to himself and given me faith. With a heart filled with amazement and praise, I gladly acknowledged that I owed every part of my salvation to God's grace in sovereign election. I knew I was in possession of eternal life only because the Father had chosen me, the Saviour had died for me, and the Holy Spirit had given me faith and a new heart.'

When John Reisinger finished his studies in Lancaster he went to his first pastoral charge in Lewisburg. There he discovered the practical consequences of believing in election. One morning during his personal devotions, he read these words, 'For who maketh thee to differ from another? And what hast thou that thou didst not receive? now if thou didst receive it, why dost thou glory, as if thou hadst not received it?' (*1 Cor.* 4:7). Several providences were to happen to John that day which convinced him of the authority of those words, and this is one:

'I was standing on the steps of the Post Office opening my mail. Suddenly I heard a man calling my name and interjecting a curse or two in between shouts. It was an old Navy buddy I had not seen for over twelve years. He slapped me on the back, and with unprintable language, told me how glad he was to see me. He proceeded to pull me towards a local tavern for a drink. I will never forget the look on his face when I told him what the Lord Jesus Christ had done in my life and that I was now a pastor. The blank look turned into a big grin which was followed by a loud laugh. "Boy, that's the best one I ever heard. You almost had me fooled. Now you blankety-blank, tell me the truth. No more wild stories. What have you been doing with yourself?" I finally had to take my friend down the street and show him my name on the outside bulletin board of the church before he would believe me.

'As he walked away shaking his head, the Lord again reminded me, "Who maketh thee to differ?" I knew my friend and I were both alike by nature. Scenes of past sins we had committed together raced through my mind, sins in which we had equally rejoiced to revel. But something had happened to change all that. He still loved that kind of life and those same sins, but I now hated both the sins and their very remembrance. The memory of my wilful ignorance and unbelief in being a willing slave to such things filled me with shame.

'As the man walked away shaking his head, I again felt tears on my cheeks. I was different from him, and yet I was no different at all. By nature and practice I had been just as sinful and just as guilty. But not any longer. I had been changed. What had made the difference? If you would have said to me at that moment, "Well, John, it is all because you were willing to accept Christ and he was not", I would have said, "Nothing could be further from the truth." I knew then, and pray that God will never let me forget it, that nothing less than the sovereign grace of God in electing love was the sole cause of my difference. Let others boast about what they have accomplished by the power of their mighty will. I shall gladly lay all the glory of my salvation at the feet of free and sovereign grace. It was the Lord who "made me to differ". It was surely not my free will.'

John Reisinger now believed in God's unconditional election, and also in the depravity of man's nature. In addition he believed that all whom the Father had given to the Son would persevere to the very end, kept by the power of God. He had heard that there were those who believed that the purpose of Christ's death was effectually to redeem all that vast number whom the Father had given to the Son, and thus that the atonement was limited in its design (although not in its power) for them. Once again there were clear verses that taught that truth: 'Thou shalt call his name JESUS, for he shall save his people from their sins' (*Matt.* 1:21); 'I am the good shepherd; the good shepherd giveth his life for the sheep' (*John* 10:11); 'Feed the church of God, which he hath purchased with his own blood' (*Acts* 20:28); 'God shows his love for us in that while we were yet sinners Christ died for us' (*Rom.* 5:8); 'For if while we were enemies we were reconciled to God by the death of his Son, much more, now that we are reconciled, shall we be saved by his life' (*Rom.* 5:10); 'Christ also loved the church, and gave himself for it; That he might sanctify and cleanse it with the washing of water by the word, that he might present it to himself a glorious church, not having spot or wrinkle, or any such thing; but that it might be holy and without blemish' (*Eph.* 5:25–27); 'He gave himself for us in order that he might redeem us from all iniquity and purify to himself a people for his own possession, zealous of good works' (*Titus* 2:14).

But John Reisinger had many questions about this teaching. Would embracing it restrain a Christian's evangelistic concern? What of those verses in the Bible that talked of 'the world' and 'all' and taught that it was not God's will that any should perish? It was at that time, that there came into the congregation in Lewisburg an elderly man named I. C. Herendeen, whom we have already mentioned. He had a tract and book ministry called 'Bible Truth Depot' that barely supported him. In earlier years he had been a friend of Arthur Pink. Herendeen began to sit under John's ministry in 1953 (the year after Arthur Pink died in the Hebrides) and soon he was writing encouraging letters to John on most Mondays. Two or three pages in length, the letters sometimes raised questions he was not able to answer, and they sent John back to the Bible. Herendeen was wise and patient. He heard John quoting from C. H. Spurgeon, and so he gave him Spurgeon's sermons and autobiographical materials addressing those theological issues where John was finding some difficulty.

Spurgeon said this:

'Some people love the doctrine of universal atonement because they say, "It is so beautiful. It is a lovely idea that Christ should die for all men; it commends itself to the instincts of humanity"; they say, "There is something in it full of joy and beauty." I admit there is; but beauty may be often associated with falsehood. There is much which I admire in the theory of universal atonement, but I will just show what the supposition necessarily involves. If Christ on his cross intended to save every man, then he intended to save those who were lost before he died. If the doctrine be true, that he died for all men, then he died for some who were in hell before he came into this world, for doubtless there were even then myriads there who had been cast away because of their sins.

'Once again, if it were Christ's intention to save all men, how deplorably has he been disappointed. For we have his own testimony that there is a lake which burneth with fire and brimstone, and into that pit of woe have been cast some of the very persons who, according to the theory of universal redemption, were bought with his blood. That seems to me a conception a thousand times more repulsive than any of those consequences which are said to be associated with the Calvinistic and Christian doctrine of special and particular redemption. To think that my Saviour died for men who were or are in hell, seems a supposition too horrible for me to entertain. To imagine for a moment that he was the Substitute for all the sons of men, and that God, having first punished the Substitute, afterwards punished the sinners themselves, seems to conflict with all my ideas of Divine justice. That Christ should offer an atonement and satisfaction for the sins of all men, and that afterwards some of those very men should be punished for the sins for which Christ had already atoned, appears to me to be the most monstrous iniquity that could ever have been imputed to Saturn, to Janus, to the goddess of the Thugs, or to the most diabolical heathen deities. God forbid that we should ever think thus of Jehovah, the Just and wise and good!'[1]

The issue concerning the purpose and extent of the atonement of Christ is that, unless we believe that mankind without exception is ultimately going to be in heaven, we cannot have an unlimited atonement. If we universalize the extent of the atonement and cry, 'Yes, he died in the place of every single person in the whole history of the world', then we limit the power of the blood of Christ because many of those people have perished. His blood was too diluted to save them all. Such teachers are limiting the efficacy of the blood of Christ to save those whom he tried in vain to redeem. We shall have none of it. All Christ died to save – that countless vast multitude – shall indeed be saved by his precious blood.

So it was the Bible that persuaded John Reisinger of God's sovereign grace in election and atonement, helped by the writings of men like Charles Haddon Spurgeon and the personal counsel of I. C. Herendeen. John came to believe in those old Protestant teachings, which men have come to call, 'The Five Points of Calvinism,' that is, Total Depravity, Unconditional

[1] C. H. Spurgeon's *Autobiography*, vol. 1, 1834–54, London: Passmore & Alabaster, 1897 (revised edition, London: Banner of Truth, 1962), Chapter 16, *A Defence of Calvinism*, p. 175.

Election, Limited Atonement, Irresistible Grace and the Perseverance of the Saints. On John's frequent visits to Carlisle he would share his biblical pilgrimage with his brother Ernie and with other members of Grace Chapel. It was John who gave Ernie his first copy of a book published by the Banner of Truth Trust, when it was reprinted in 1960. It was Brownlow North's *The Rich Man and Lazarus*. He and I. C. Herendeen also spoke to other thinking men and women in the congregation. Duke Irwin was then a deacon and he saw those truths and embraced them. He and his wife were to become most involved in the church's book table.

The pastor at Grace Chapel from 1952 was Robert H. Depp, and he soon received this teaching which gave such honour and glory to God. The implications of the sovereignty of God for evangelism, worship and sanctification overwhelmed him. He began to teach them from the pulpit far too clearly and frequently for cautious Ernie to appreciate, and he made a luncheon appointment with the young preacher. So Robert Depp got prepared for a confrontation. 'Bob,' Ernie said at the table, 'you are tuned to the right channel, but you've got the volume up too loud.'

From a surprising source Robert Depp had received some additional encouragements to embrace the truths of God's free grace. His sister-in-law's 'Uncle Sidney' turned out to be S. M. Houghton, a history teacher in Wales, who was connected with the *Banner of Truth* magazine (Oxford) almost from its outset in 1955. Later Houghton worked as an editor of Banner of Truth publications for many years. A lively correspondence developed between the two men, with Houghton recommending and supplying books. And again another rich source of literature came to this young preacher when he was given the library of a deceased Presbyterian minister with many fine old books. But while Depp preached these newly-discovered truths with enthusiasm, there was occasionally a little polemicism to mar the sermons.

Why was Reisinger initially cool towards Calvinism? Bob Depp attributed it to three factors:

First, Ernie was above all else a soul-winner, an avid witness for Christ. In those years in Carlisle of their first love for the Lord Christ and his truth it was not uncommon for Bob Depp to be awakened at all hours of the night by phone calls from Ernie, 'Pastor, can you come on over and explain the gospel to this person to whom I have been witnessing.' No doubt Ernie must have given some credibility to the common warnings that Calvinism kills evangelism. Ernie himself says, 'I fought against what I thought they were teaching. I thought it would kill evangelism, kill the prayer meeting, and would lead to fatalism.'

Secondly, Ernie was a voracious reader, and a feature of the 1950s was the proliferation of Arminian literature. Few books made the doctrines of grace accessible to the inquirer.

Thirdly, Carlisle and its neighbouring towns were regularly visited by fundamentalist preachers from Philadelphia. These men were not sympathetic to the rediscovery of historic Christianity, rather they sounded an alarm about the consequences to the church of this occurrence. Some of them spoke at Grace Chapel, and there were members of the congregation who would say, 'If Dr So-and-so and his colleagues believe that way, how can we say such great men of God are wrong?'

Yet what happened in Carlisle, as in so many other places, was that these truths actually won over the congregation, though Robert Depp was almost destroyed in the process. He resigned as pastor in 1956 because he felt ill-equipped to deal with the controversy that had developed within the church.

He believed he needed to go back to seminary and do some study in depth. He also ended up in hospital with a perforated ulcer. His wife Janie quipped, 'Your faith in a sovereign God is in your head, but it hasn't reached your stomach yet.' But at the next deacons' meeting the deacons, including Ernie, did a complete turnabout and acknowledged that they too had come to embrace these truths, asking Bob to stay on and pastor the church. But his plans were complete, and it was time for the Depps to leave Carlisle.

What factors made Ernie lay hold of these truths without any reservation, and become their champion? Firstly, he appreciated the preaching of the minister of Tenth Presbyterian Church in Philadelphia, Dr Donald Grey Barnhouse. Barnhouse believed in the doctrines of grace and through his ministry a deacon and a deacon's wife in Grace Chapel had been converted. Secondly, and more significantly, Ernie believed in the complete authority and absolute perfection of Scripture. If the Scriptures plainly said something, that settled it for him. Finally, he had strong distaste for phoniness, hypocrisy and professionalism in ministry. A phrase he might use in praying was, 'Lord make us real, one hundred percent wool and a yard wide!' Those humbling and God-exalting truths of Calvinism stripped away any false veneers and caused men to see their rebellious hearts in the light of God's holiness. They demand a divine effectual work if salvation is to be applied to a sinner. There is no doubt about it, when God laid hold of Ernest Reisinger and brought him low those many years earlier in the Aberdeen Proving Ground in Maryland, he raised him up a new creation.

Ernest Reisinger put his change of mind in his own way:

'I came to Calvinism kicking, fighting and screaming. There is yet more mercy in God than there was rebellion and ignorance in me. Grace proved to be irresistible. Why? Because grace subdued my power to resist. 'Blessed is the man you choose and cause to approach unto you' (*Psa.* 65:4). I got a new Bible, a new message of evangelism, and also some new methods in evangelism. Believing in grace did not leave me passive or inert. No, the very opposite took place. Grace did not regard me as a piece of wood, or a tin can, or a robot. It took possession of me. Grace did not annihilate my powers, rather it removed my powerlessness. Grace did not destroy my will, but freed it from sin. Now, when I sing 'Amazing Grace', I know what John Newton really meant. Duke Irwin and I, the most active leaders in the church at that time, steadily led the congregation into the main stream of historical and biblical Christianity.'

These changes took place in the first years of Grace Baptist Church in Carlisle. It has now persevered in those doctrines of grace for half a century with scarcely any variation. The only change is that now the congregation is three or four times as large as it was forty years ago.

9

THEOLOGICAL GROWTH

While Ernest Reisinger was developing in his understanding of the sovereignty of God and what salvation by grace alone meant, he was also being challenged concerning the 'dispensationalist' approach to the Bible which he had been taught. In the United States of America the largest network of congregations is that which holds to the dispensationalist understanding of the Bible. Dispensationalism divides the Bible up into periods of time during which, it claims, mankind was tested in respect to different specific revelations of the will of God. These dispensations differ from or even contradict one another. The seven stated in the Scofield Reference Bible are: Innocence, Conscience, Human Government, Promise, Law, Grace and Kingdom.

The dispensationalist pulpits of America are supported by such a famous school as Dallas Theological Seminary and maintained by many other Bible Schools and Colleges found in almost every state in the nation. For example, near Carlisle is Philadelphia College of the Bible and also Lancaster Bible College. The thousands of assemblies of the Plymouth Brethren, the Independent Baptists, the Assemblies of God and all the other Pentecostal churches, the Conservative Baptists, the Regular Baptists, most charismatic fellowships, and many missionary societies share a dispensationalist and so a pre-millennial confession of faith. This is the face of American evangelicalism, and multitudes of true followers of the Lord Jesus equate this attitude to the Bible with Christianity.

They are taught that God had two totally distinct plans for history: one concerning an earthly people, Israel, and the other concerning a heavenly people, the church. God's plan for Israel pointed to the establishment of a Messianic kingdom on the earth, but Israel's rejection of Christ resulted in God's postponement of that kingdom, his turning away from Israel and his creating out of the Gentiles a new people, the church. When God has finished building the church he will rapture it secretly to heaven and then resume his dealings with Israel. That will be followed by the events of the last days, the great tribulation, the battle of Armageddon, the Second Coming of Christ, the binding of Satan and the setting up of the millennial kingdom.

The struggle Ernie had experienced in embracing the doctrines of grace was of briefer duration than the years he spent wondering about the dispensationalist view of the Bible and whether it could be supported by the Scriptures themselves. Paul E. Sisco wrote thus of his own experience:

'I was an ardent dispensationalist. Since I was twenty years of age I read and studied the Scofield Reference Bible, books, pamphlets and tracts which taught me this new system of Bible interpretation. My one desire after I came to Christ was to understand the Word of God and to teach others what I had learned. I took advantage of every opportunity to hear many teachers, preachers and lecturers who proclaimed the so-called dispensational pre-millennial approach for proper study and understanding the Bible. Fifteen years of my life were devoted to preaching and teaching the Word of God. Obviously, I taught as I was taught. I expounded to others the "distinctive" teachings of dispensationalism.'[1]

Those were also Ernie's beginnings. He says:

'I spent the first ten years of my life immersed in dispensationalism. I wore out three Scofield Bibles, and the fourth was falling apart. I had heard Lewis Sperry Chafer in person. The only systematic theology I had studied was Dr Chafer's eight-volume set which was hot from the press in 1947. The formative years of my spiritual development were under the ministry of Christian men committed to dispensationalism. It was under such a ministry that I was taught the importance of a personal devotional life, the fundamentals of the faith, to be missionary minded and a personal witness for Christ. One of the first books that had an effect on my evangelism was *True Evangelism* by Lewis Sperry Chafer. I can still recommend much in that book . . . I would not be disrespectful or uncharitable to many genuine Christians who hold to this view, though I now consider it to be erroneous and dangerous. Although I strongly differ from my dispensationalist brethren in their interpretation of Scripture, I do not wish to separate from their fellowship. No Christian wishes to be argumentative, yet I strongly believe it to be a departure from the historic faith of our fathers.'

Ernest Reisinger was reading widely from leading men of God in church history, and he was not finding dispensationalist teachings in one of them. That fact became increasingly perplexing. That awareness was what made Paul E. Sisco rethink his position:

[1] Paul E. Sisco, *Scofield or the Scriptures*, Chapel Library, Box 1335, Venice, Florida 33595, no date, p. 5.

'Why did not men of God in the past who wrote church history, commentaries, theological textbooks, concordances and sermons, teach the same? Surely they were scholars and should have known. But how strange it was that they failed to possess and teach the "light" of dispensationalism. They did not mention a restored Jewish political state or a thousand-year reign of Christ on David's literal throne in a natural and material kingdom. They seemed to be absolutely unaware of a so-called kingdom postponement, a future national Jewish restoration, a transitional or parenthetical period, three gospels, two or three future resurrections, three future judgments and many other interrelated doctrines. Possibly they were just old-fashioned, and though they were in earnest and sincere, the "light" of dispensationalism had not dawned upon them and they knew not how to "rightly divide the word of truth". This reasoning, however, did not satisfy my mind and heart nor clear my conscience. As I read and studied the Bible I became confused and convicted of gross misinterpretations of many truths that a child could understand.'

Paul Sisco is correct in highlighting the absence of the dispensationalist approach to the Bible in confessions of faith, commentaries and Bible dictionaries of historic Christianity. The Plymouth Brethren movement claimed from its very beginning around 1830 that its teaching represented a wide departure from the doctrines of its predecessors and contemporaries. According to them, theologians and commentators like John Calvin, Matthew Henry and Matthew Poole were deluded by 'man-made doctrines'. Only the Brethren were subject and submissive to the Bible as the Word of God. Oswald Smith also discredited those earlier Christian writers: 'I know very few of the old commentaries that are trustworthy when it comes to prophecy. Nearly all of them spiritualize the predictions of the Old Testament prophets and confuse the kingdom with the Church. Hence their interpretations are worthless.'[1] That writer also quoted Isaiah 11 and 12 and declared, 'None of it was fulfilled at the first advent, and none of it can be spiritualized, for it has no fulfilment in the Church, in spite of what the great commentators say. God did not see fit to enlighten them.'[2]

The Scofield Bible also acknowledged that its approach is very different from that of historic Christianity, since the old teaching was untrustworthy. The reader of the Scofield Bible is told that as he studies the Gospels he must free his mind from the belief that the church is the true Israel, and that the Old Testament foreview of the kingdom is fulfilled in the church. Scofield admitted that this 'notion' was 'a legacy in Protestant thought'.[3]

Dispensationalists teach that the church was not prophesied in the Old Testament. Harry Ironside, one time pastor of the Moody Memorial Church in Chicago, boasted that this opinion was nonexistent until introduced by J. N. Darby in the nineteenth century:

'In fact, until brought to the fore through the writings and preaching of a distinguished ex-clergyman, Mr J. N. Darby, in the early part of the last century, it is scarcely to be found in a single book or sermon throughout a period of 1600 years! If any doubt this statement, let them search, as the writer has in a measure done, the remarks of the so-called Fathers, both pre- and post-Nicene, the theological treatises of the scholastic divines, Roman Catholic writers of all shades of thought, the literature of the Reformation, the sermons and expositions

[1] Oswald J. Smith, *When the King Comes Back*, p. 13.

[2] *ibid*. p. 63. [3] *Scofield Bible*, 1917 ed., p. 989.

of the Puritans, and the general theological works of the day. He will find the "mystery" conspicuous by its absence.'[1]

Dispensationalism taught the 'parenthesis theory' of the kingdom and the church. According to this approach, the church age is an unforeseen parenthesis in God's 'Jewish programme' as described by Old Testament prophets. If the Jews had not rejected the Lord Jesus as the Messiah, the Jewish kingdom would have begun at our Lord's first coming. But God's 'Plan A' failed, or was thwarted or interrupted, and the church age, totally unforeseen by the Old Testament prophets, was interjected as 'Plan B', a substitute for 'Plan A'. The dispensationalists call the whole life of the church in the last two thousand years the 'parenthetical church age'.

Reisinger's spirit of self-sufficiency had been humbled by the Sovereign Lord. It was by God's grace that he had been conquered, in all his long rebellion against the Saviour. To him this parenthesis theory of the kingdom of God and the church displayed an inadequate attitude to the Almighty. Who could judge the God of the Bible powerless to perform any plan which he has determined? Is he not sovereign in creation, in redemption and in providence? The living God is all-wise and omnipotent in both planning and accomplishing his will. Dispensationalist teachers have to face the implications of their parenthesis theory: it sets limits upon the illimitable God. If our life today in God's church is in a mere parenthesis, when did this begin, and how is it known? When will it end, and how is this to be known?

Another weak link in dispensational thought is its false antithesis between the law and the gospel. 'During the Mosaic

[1] Harry A. Ironside, *Mysteries of God*, Loizeaux Brothers, no date, p. 50.

dispensation God dealt with men by law', says the dispensationalist, 'while today he deals with men by grace.' A footnote of the Scofield Bible claims, 'Grace . . . is, therefore, constantly set in contrast to law, under which God demands righteousness from man, whereas under grace he gives righteousness to man. Law is connected with Moses and works; grace with Christ and faith. As a dispensation grace begins with the death and resurrection of Christ. The point of testing is no longer legal obedience, but acceptance or rejection of Christ.' Scofield further claimed that 'Scripture never, in any dispensation, mingles these two principles. Everywhere the Scriptures present law and grace in sharply contrasted spheres'.

How different was the attitude to the law displayed in those Christian writings which had now become Reisinger's delight. Spurgeon, having witnessed the emergence and spread of J. N. Darby's views, commented, 'Very great mistakes have been made about the law. Not long ago there were those about us who affirmed that the law is utterly abrogated and abolished, and they openly taught that believers were not bound to make the moral law a rule for their lives. What would have been sin in other men, they counted as no sin in themselves. From such Antinomianism as that, may the Lord deliver us. We are not under the law as the method of salvation, but we delight to see the law in the hand of Christ, and desire to obey the Lord in all things.'[2]

The Puritans and their heirs did not contrast law and grace, as do the dispensationalists, but they set law over against gospel, both under the canopy of grace, with grace working

[1] *Scofield Reference Bible*, 1917 ed., p. 1115.

[2] Charles Haddon Spurgeon, *Metropolitan Tabernacle Pulpit*, Volume 28, Sermon 1660.

by the instrumentality both of the law and of the gospel. What, then, is the purpose of the law? It prepares us for Christ. This must be true in three distinct senses:

Firstly, *the moral law convicts us all of sin*; of commands transgressed, of demands disregarded. So it drives us to the need for forgiveness (that is, grace) as our only hope. Sin – in the sense of falling short of God's eternal standard – has reigned ever since the Fall, but sin only becomes conscious transgression in the light of law. In one of Reisinger's favourite books, William Guthrie's *The Christian's Great Interest*, the author points out that though God may call some from the womb, some in a sovereign gospel way, some in the hour of death, his most ordinary way is by a prior law-work. The good news is only good news to those who have heard the bad news. Even the ceremonial law of the Old Testament always pointed the awakened sinner to the possibility of grace, but it was grace in the semblance and shackles of law; and Calvary, where grace stands fully revealed, represents a wonderful liberation from these exacting and meticulous demands. But Israel as a whole stumbled, in both Old and New Testaments. Instead of being driven by the moral law to take refuge in grace through the ceremonial law, the Jews erected out of the moral and ceremonial law together a false way of self-righteousness. So they missed the very purpose of both laws, and refused to submit themselves to the gift of righteousness in Christ.

Secondly, *the moral law reveals* not only human failure and transgression, but *the essential sinfulness and rebellion of the human heart*. Thus it drives us to regeneration (that is, grace) as the only remedy. It is not merely that men have not kept the law; they have not so much as wanted to keep it, but have rebelled against it. So men do not only need forgiveness, but cleansing of heart, the new birth, a radical change in their innermost beings. There is, of course, something of this in the Old Testament. It was typified, in part, by the laver of the ceremonial law; and it was apprehended by faith by David (Psalm 51). But chiefly, in the Old Testament, it was depicted as characteristic of the New Covenant, in such passages as Jeremiah 31:31–34 and Ezekiel 36:33–36. This New Covenant was to include heart cleansing, a commandment written on the heart and mind, signifying the glad response to its dictates of one who has been regenerated in will, affections and outlook. It was thus that the apostle could write, 'For I delight in the law of God after the inward man' (*Rom.* 7:22).

Thirdly, *the moral law continues to reveal sin in the believer* even after this experience of regeneration, and so *drives him continually to seek renewed forgiveness and sanctifying power* (that is, grace). The apostle John tells us that 'If we say that we have no sin, we deceive ourselves', but if we 'confess our sins, he is faithful and just to forgive us our sins, and to cleanse us from all unrighteousness.' And the apostle Paul, after saying that he delights in the law of God after the inward man, adds, 'But I see another law in my members, warring against the law of my mind, and bringing me into captivity to the law of sin which is in my members' (*Rom.* 7:23). For this situation the New Testament reveals only one remedy, when the apostle continues, 'For the law of the Spirit of life in Christ Jesus hath made me free from the law of sin and death. For what the law could not do, in that it was weak through the flesh, God sending his own Son in the likeness of sinful flesh, and for sin condemned sin in the flesh: that the righteousness of the law might be fulfilled in us, who walk not after the flesh, but after the Spirit' (*Rom* 8:2–4). So the law makes Christ more precious to believers.

One of the contributions that Ernie Reisinger has made to the contemporary church has been his plea that evangelical Christians rediscover the place of the law. He has been convinced that a new and more powerful proclamation of that law is one of the most pressing needs of the hour. Men would have less difficulty with the gospel if only they learned the lesson of the law. So it always is: a low view of law always brings legalism in religion; a high view of law makes a man a seeker after grace. Reisinger ends one of his books on the law of God with these words:

'If the whole human race had kept the Ten Commandments, not violating one, the law would not stand in so splendid a position of honour as it does today when the man Christ Jesus has rendered satisfaction to it. God incarnate has in his life, and yet more in his death, revealed the supremacy of the law; he has shown that not even sovereignty can set aside justice. Who shall say a word against the law to which the Lawgiver himself submits? God the Father demanded the perfection of the law from his own dear Son . . . Before I conclude, let me issue a solemn call and invitation to all the poor lawbreakers who read these words. Be sure of this, you will not get to heaven by keeping the commandments; you are a guilty lawbreaker and need pardon, forgiveness, and mercy. Any serious consideration of the Ten Commandments will make every honest person cry out, "Oh, the load of guilt that is on my soul! My head and my heart are full of sin. Oh, my sins! Every commandment takes hold upon me; how great then is the sum of my guilt!"

'The commandments should cause every lawbreaker to cry out, "Come, Lord Jesus. Come quickly to my rescue. Save me, Lord, or I will perish."

'Only Christ can save you from the hand of justice. He alone will be your protection from the arm of the law. If you have any pity for your poor, perishing soul, close with the present offers of mercy. Do not shut the doors of mercy against yourself, but rather repent and be converted.'[1]

[1] Ernest C. Reisinger, *Whatever Happened to the Ten Commandments?*, Edinburgh: Banner of Truth, 1999, pp. 108–9).

10

VICTORIOUS CHRISTIAN LIVING

ERNIE REISINGER MADE ADDITIONAL ADVANCE in his understanding of the Christian life when he became increasingly suspicious of the claims of those who believed that by one experience they had entered a higher plane of victorious Christian living. In this regard he again parted company with dispensationalism which espouses the so-called 'carnal Christian' teaching popularized in the notes of the *Scofield Reference Bible*. A statement from those notes indicates the precise nature of the teaching: 'Paul divides men into three classes: "Natural", i.e. the Adamic man, unrenewed through the new birth; "Spiritual", i.e. the renewed man as Spirit-filled and walking in the Spirit in full communion with God; "Carnal", "fleshly", i.e. the renewed man who, walking "after the flesh", remains a babe in Christ.'[1]

It is very important, Reisinger observes, to observe two of the claims of these Scofield notes: first, the division of men into three classes, and second, that one of these classes of men comprises a whole category of believers known as the 'carnal', the 'fleshly', 'the babe(s) in Christ', 'those who walk after the

[1] *Scofield Reference Bible*, 1917 ed., pp. 1213–14.

flesh'. To 'walk' implies the *bent* of their lives; their leaning or bias is in one direction, that is, towards carnality.

By contrast, the Bible knows of just two classes of men, sheep and goats, saved and lost, those on a narrow way to life and others on a broad road to destruction. It knows nothing of a third class of men saved, because they have made some kind of decision about Christ, but behaving in every way like the world. Who were these Corinthian Christians who were yet behaving carnally? Certainly they were imperfectly sanctified men and women, as are all Christians, but Paul is not saying that they were characterized by carnality in every area of their lives. He was not expounding a general doctrine of carnality but reproving a specific outcropping of carnality in one specific respect.

When the Corinthians displayed a party spirit and aligned themselves with Cephas or Paul, boasting in their favourite's prowess, then they were acting carnally and not spiritually. David's carnality was his conduct with Bathsheba; Noah's carnality was his bout of excess drinking; Peter's carnality was his oaths at the fireside. These men were not carnal in the whole drift of their lives. They were not members of a third 'class' of mankind when they fell into those sins. They were children of God behaving inconsistently – as every believer can do. What Scofield has done is to allow the church to rationalize an easy-believism and decisionism by placing such former professors of faith – who proceed to show no interest in Christianity – inside the kingdom of heaven, but labelling them as 'carnal Christians'. What they need, Scofield goes on to say, is a second work of grace.

The 'carnal Christian' teaching is the mother of many second-work-of-grace errors that uniformly depreciate biblical conversion by implying that the change in the converted sinner may amount to little or nothing. It goes on to say that *the* important change which affects a man's character and conduct is the subsequent second step (which he himself, once again, freely decides to take). This makes him a 'spiritual Christian'.

The 'carnal Christian' teaching is therefore the mother of one of the most soul-destroying teachings of our day. It suggests that you can take Jesus as your Saviour and yet treat obedience to his lordship as *optional*. How often is the appeal made to the so-called 'carnal Christians' to go on, and put Jesus on the throne and 'make him Lord'! When they have accepted Jesus as Lord, they are told that they will cease to be 'carnal Christians'. But in the New Testament Christ is always presented as Lord. Ernie discovered the Puritan commentator Matthew Henry saying, 'Unless we consent to him as our Lord we cannot expect any benefit by him as our Saviour.' Such conviction characterizes all Reformation and Puritan authors. The word 'Saviour' occurs only twice in the Acts of the Apostles; on the other hand the title 'Lord' appears ninety-two times. The gospel is, 'Believe on the *Lord* Jesus Christ and thou shalt be saved.'

Then gradual and effectual growth in grace, knowledge, faith, love, and holiness follows. All this the Bible clearly teaches, and it is exemplified in the life of true Christians. The Bible urges us to 'pursue holiness' (*Heb*. 12:14). To *pursue* is not passive. To pursue means personal exertion as well as faith. The apostle Paul expresses the pursuit of sanctification in such terms as 'I run', 'I war', 'I keep under my body', and 'Let us labour', and 'Let us lay aside every weight'. 'Trust God and get going', is the message of the Bible, rather than, 'Let go and let God'. Claims to instantaneous leaps from conversion to consecration by an act of faith do not find support from the

Bible, and conversion itself has been demeaned by it. Need anything divine and eternal happen with such a low view of regeneration? One scarcely thinks that people who have made a mental assent to the invitations of the gospel have been actually converted. The stress on the necessity of the second work of God can depress the weak while inflating the egos of the shallow and ignorant.

The working of God's Spirit in our hearts on earth and the cleansing of our sins by Christ's blood in heaven are inseparably joined together in the application of God's salvation. Justification and sanctification always go together in salvation. Any attempt to place the basic act of submission to Christ after conversion cuts the vital nerve of the new covenant and perverts biblical Christianity. To separate these blessings which God has joined together in one covenant is to bring dishonour on the blood that was shed to enact the entirety of the new covenant.

Ernest Reisinger's journey to these convictions was longer than the one he took to embrace the Reformed faith, with many blind alleys having to be explored on the way. Early in his Christian life he was given Hannah Whitall Smith's book, *The Christian's Secret of a Happy Life*, first published in 1875. What this book was holding out to him was happiness and victory over sin. What Christian would not desire that? Ernie followed all the instructions in the book, and for short periods thought he actually had gained the victory, only to return to the inward struggle against remaining sin. Yet he continued to seek this complete victory that was being promised by Smith.

Then a friend who knew that Ernie was seeking a more holy life suggested that he attend a conference held annually in the heart of New York city on Thirteenth Street at A. B. Simpson's former Christian and Missionary Alliance Church. So Ernie packed his bags and travelled to New York, renting a room in a nearby hotel. The speaker was an Englishman, Ian Thomas, and he spoke on the first night on 'The Man in Romans 7'. He announced that the next night he was going to speak on how to get out of Romans 7 into Romans 8. The first night's message on Romans 7 had described Ernie perfectly and he could not wait for the next night. Ernie was longing and seeking to get out of Romans 7. The Christian in Romans 7, according to the Scofield Reference Bible, is 'the experience of the renewed man, under the law, and still ignorant of the delivering power of the Holy Spirit.'[1]

Ian Thomas described the victorious living of the man in Romans 8 on the second evening, and for the remainder of the conference Ernie went back to his room and cried to God that the Lord would give him that victory over sin, translating him from being the defeated man of Romans 7 to being the triumphant man of Romans 8. Ernie made an appointment to see Ian Thomas privately in order that the speaker might usher him into becoming the 'Romans 8 Man', but neither preaching nor personal counsel were of any avail. Thomas told Ernie that he was leaving New York for Chicago to speak at 'Founders Week' at Moody Bible Institute in Chicago. Ernie called his wife and told her about Ian Thomas and the victorious life that he was promising. To be in such a spiritual state would be worth anything in the world: 'Oh, to be out of Romans 7 and into Romans 8!' So Ernie set off to Chicago to get that blessing. There he again met with Ian Thomas and heard him preach on these same themes. He also met one of his associates, but again neither private nor public counsels availed and Ernie left Chicago at the end of 'Founders Week'

[1] *Scofield Reference Bible*, 1917 ed., p. 1200.

just as he had come there, still in Romans 7. Now, about forty years later, Ernie is still in Romans 7 and also in Romans 8, for now he understands his state much better, and knows that a Christian lives in both chapters at once.

The law of God has given to Ernest Reisinger a knowledge of his sin, and that is Romans 7. The gospel has given him a knowledge of the way of salvation, and that is Romans 8. He needs both, because he lives in both in this life. That Reisinger is 'carnal, sold under sin', is true, but it is not the whole truth about him. What the law does for Ernie is to give him knowledge of his true condition, and every Christian is thankful for such a truthful diagnosis and flees from any words that would ignore the evaluation.

When Ernie reviews his life by the light of the law he always finds that he has done less than the good he wanted to do; thus he 'finds' and 'sees' that sin is still in him, and that he is still to a degree taken captive by it (*Rom.* 7:21–23). How delighted he is that he also lives with the assurance that through Christ there is no condemnation (*Rom.* 8:1). The wretchedness of the 'wretched man' thus springs from the discovery of Ernie's continuing sinfulness, and the knowledge that he cannot hope to be rid of indwelling sin, his troublesome inmate, while he remains in the body. He is painfully conscious that for the present his reach exceeds his grasp, and therefore he longs for the great deliverance which is now not far away from him. Only upon his death and entrance into his Saviour's presence will the tension of Romans 7 and Romans 8, of achievement and status, purpose and performance, plan and action be abolished.[1] Summarizing this subject, Reisinger has said:

[1] See J. I. Packer, *Keep in Step with the Spirit* (IVP, 1984, pp. 263–70.

'How I wish everyone who heard the words, "This is my blood of the new covenant", would know, experience, and understand the blessings and benefits of that covenant. Then all would realize that there is no justification without sanctification, no forgiveness without growth in grace, no new standing with God without a new walk with God, no having Jesus as Saviour without also having him as Lord.

'The non-Lordship teachers do not agree that justification and sanctification, though distinguishable doctrines, are inseparably joined together in the application of God's salvation. They make sanctification optional; a justified person may or may not be sanctified, i.e. "Live the Christian life". But if God ever gives you salvation, be sure that holiness will be a part of it. If Christ does not wash you from the filth of sin, you have no part with him. Jesus said to Peter, "If I do not wash you, you have no part with me" (*John* 13:8). It is a strange kind of salvation that does not produce a desire for purity and holiness. Such a salvation was never purchased by the blood of Christ. "He will save his people *from* their sins" (*Matt.* 1:21). The Puritan Thomas Adams said, "They know not Christ who seek to divide his blood from his water, and they shall fail in justification in heaven that refuse sanctification on earth."

'There are many reasons why this truth should concern every serious Christian.

· It involves true conversion.

· It bears directly on the many self-deceived church members who have walked aisles, troubled baptismal waters, signed decision cards, and had their names entered on church rolls, yet who give no biblical evidence of Holy Ghost regeneration. Can a serious person look at present-day church members and not be moved with holy concern and compassion?

· It puts repentance back into the evangelistic message.

· It deals a death blow to all second-work-of-grace teachings, such as the "higher life", the "crucified life" and the "deeper life", which represents a wrong view of salvation: "Let go and let God."

· It should settle the lordship controversy by putting to rest the notion that Jesus as Saviour is little more than a hell-insurance policy, and the obedience is optional.

'The Bible knows nothing about a justified man in whom sanctification has not begun. Nor does the Bible know anything of a sanctified man who has not been justified. The Bible says that without holiness (sanctification) no man will see the Lord (*Heb.* 12:14). This refers not to a positional sanctification, which every believer possesses once and for all in Christ. The passage is referring to personal holiness that every believer is duty-bound to pursue continually. None who fails to pursue holiness will see God's face in peace. Please note, I say, 'pursue'. Only one has attained absolute holiness. Jesus alone was perfect.

'If Christian in *Pilgrim's Progress* was only passive on his way to the Celestial City and never fought, struggled and wrestled, then I have read the immortal volume in vain – and I have read it about twenty times. But the plain truth is that man will persist in confounding two things that differ, that is, justification and sanctification. In justification the message to men is to believe – only to entrust themselves to the Lord Jesus Christ. In sanctification the message is watch, fight and pray. What God has divided let us not mingle and confuse.

'Before anyone would take a one–leap short-cut to a victorious life, may I plead with you to read John Bunyan's *Pilgrim's Progress*, and his *Holy War*, J. C. Ryle's *Holiness*, and from the sixth volume of John Owen's *Works*, 'The

Mortification of Sin', 'Temptation', 'Indwelling Sin in Believers', and his 'Exposition of Psalm 130'.

'My doctrinal views have not undergone any major change as to their truth or importance since I embraced that Pauline system of doctrine commonly called Calvinism. I pray that I have become more gracious and patient with those who hold others especially those who believe in the Ten Commandments, the Lord's Prayer, and the Apostles' Creed. My chief mentors have been men who firmly hold to the leading sentiments of Calvinism, but their spirit is like that of John Bunyan. I wish my doctrinal legacy to be expressed in some notes of William Jay written in the front of his Study Bible:

"In reading this Book, let me guard against four things –

1. the contractedness of the Systematic;
2. the mysticism of the Allegorizer;
3. the dogmatism of the Bigot;
4. the presumption of the Rationalist.

Let me tremble at God's word, and let me, in reading it, keep three purposes in view:

1. To collect facts rather than form opinions;
2. To regulate practice rather than encourage speculation;
3. To aid devotion rather than dispute."[1]

[1] *The Autobiography of William Jay*, 1854, reprinted Edinburgh: Banner of Truth, 1974, p. 171.

11

PRAYER, EVANGELISM AND BOOKS

During the 1950s, until Roger Irwin's marriage in 1956, he and Ernest Reisinger lived next door to one another. For a few years their homes were further apart, but in the 1960s they again lived close to one another at a different development. This proximity allowed them to come together to pray early in the morning every day, and they continued to do so for years until the Reisingers moved away from Carlisle. Roger was the one man with whom Ernie prayed most regularly. They often met during the spring and summer in a quiet corner of a nearby cemetery. They used an up-or-down window-shade system to signal if one of them would not be available. So during a period of ten years the lawyer and the building contractor read through the whole Bible together at that spot, and brought before God many individual and corporate needs. They were blessed times, and the Lord heard and answered their prayers.

Personal and corporate prayer undergirded the establishment and growth of the Carlisle Church. From the very beginning the Wednesday night prayer meeting was a priority amongst them, as it continues to be today. The officers also met regularly for prayer every Friday morning. Many husbands and wives prayed together each morning and evening as family devotions became a part of their lives. One cannot understand Ernie unless one takes account of the fact that he is a man of prayer. Who was converted for whom there had not been prayer? Deliverances in difficult child-birth, healings from life-threatening diseases, restorations from backsliding all occurred as members prayed. They cried to God that he would guide the church through sadness, discipline, building expansion, new officers, their Christian school, summer camps and conferences.

Reisinger produced a little pamphlet entitled *Doctrine and Devotion* in which he argued that belief and practice must be interdependent, that biblical truth must be clothed with genuine Christian experience. He wrote:

'Doctrine is to Christian experience what bones are to the body. A body without bones would be like a lump of "glob", utterly useless. Likewise, Christian experience without roots is like cut flowers stuck in the ground. They may look pleasant for a while, but ultimately they will fade. The other side of this truth must also be taken into account, that is, bones without flesh are but a dead skeleton. Doctrine without experience is useless.'

This bringing together of sound biblical doctrine and genuine Christian experience has been Ernie's longing in life. It is not enough to speak of immediate experiences of God without doctrinal knowledge. God must be worshipped in truth as well as in Spirit. Truth can be stated in real words, and when that is done there is Christian doctrine. To be a disciple of the Lord Jesus without knowing what Christ taught must be a vain quest. It is impossible to over-emphasize the importance of sound doctrine in the Christian life. Right thinking about all spiritual matters is imperative if we are to have right living. As men do not gather grapes of thorns, nor figs of thistles, so sound Christian character does not grow out of unsound doctrine. The church that neglects to teach sound biblical doctrine weakens church membership. It works against true unity. It invites instability in its fellowship. It lessens conviction and puts the brakes on vital progress in the congregation.

How must true Christian experience be tested amid so much spurious experience and religious confusion? Reisinger suggests three tests:

1. Is this professed religious experience produced by the truth plainly and faithfully presented? It must emerge from scriptural teaching, not be engendered merely by feeling, emotion or religious excitement.

2. Is this professed religious experience regulated and sustained by biblical truth?

3. Do the subjects of this professed religious experience manifest a general and cordial love of the truths of the Word of God?

Mark well that apostasy from the faith has never resulted from a prayerful and diligent submission to God's Word. If the great doctrines do not produce and develop such Christian character as true zeal, genuine holiness, self-denial, and evangelism, then those doctrines are not being held properly or else they have become an end in themselves.

Confessions of Faith like the Westminster and London Confessions or the Canons of Dort are clear expressions of the doctrinal content of the Bible, but there is one thing missing in each of them, and that is people. Reisinger once made that remark at a Banner of Truth ministers' conference in Leicester,

England. He told the two hundred preachers present that if he were marooned on a desert island, and could have only two books besides the Bible, he would choose the Westminster Confession of Faith and Bunyan's *Pilgrim's Progress*. A young minister approached him afterwards and asked why he would choose *Pilgrim's Progress*. Ernie repeated that the Confession did not have people in it, but Bunyan's gift was to enflesh the truths of the Confession in people. He later came to love the Heidelberg Catechism because of its personal warmth.

So the devotional house has to be built upon a doctrinal foundation. Christian preaching must produce new life because the gospel is a 'holy-making gospel.' It was the following quotation from Robert Murray M'Cheyne that provided Ernie with that phrase:

'It is a holy-making gospel. Without holy fruits all evidences are vain. You have awakenings, enlightenings, experiences and many due signs; but if you lack holiness you shall never see the Lord. A real desire after complete holiness is the truest mark of being born again. Jesus is a holy Saviour. He first covers the soul with his white raiment, then makes the soul glorious within – restores the lost image of God, and fills the soul with pure, heavenly holiness. Unregenerate men among you cannot bear this testimony.'

Thus the congregation in Carlisle steadily became committed to experiential Calvinism. That is what drew pulpit and pew alike to the Puritans of the seventeenth century, to such evangelists as Whitefield and Jonathan Edwards of the following century, and to the men of Princeton, of Scotland, London's Spurgeon and the South's Dabney and Thornwell in the nineteenth century.

They also came to love John Murray and Cornelius Van Til of Westminster Theological Seminary in nearby Philadelphia.

Great was their delight when Dr Martyn Lloyd-Jones visited Carlisle to speak at one of their first ministers' conferences. Joseph Hart once wrote, 'True religion's more than notion, Something must be known and felt.' The obverse of this is the truth that cold metaphysical reasoning and scientific arguments cannot be the way of spreading God's kingdom. True evangelism begins in believing the whole gospel and flows out of living its message before a watching world. The late 1950s witnessed the appearance of the first trickles of fine literature which were going to spread out into the world during the next forty years. Reisinger would no longer have to use a book like Paley's *Evidences* as an evangelistic tool to bring the gospel to a student. He would have a host of sharper weapons from which to choose.

The students at Dickinson College were amongst the first to benefit from these books. Ernie spent many hours having students in his home for Bible studies. One of Dickinson's former law undergraduates, Tom Martin, now a lawyer and judge, can remember luncheons at the Reisingers' apartment in an atmosphere of theological discussion. Ernie was a dairy farmer, a building contractor and a lay preacher who could yet lucidly and endearingly make old truths shine. Tom Martin recollects:

'I can remember Ernie Reisinger reading to us from *Pilgrim's Progress* those most striking and unexpected answers to questions which Christian asked Hopeful: 'Did you go to God as you had been bidden?' Hopeful answered, 'Yes, over, and over, and over.' Christian asked, 'And did the Father reveal his Son in you?' Hopeful answered, 'Not at the first, nor second, nor third, nor fourth, nor fifth, no, not at the sixth time neither.' Christian further asked, 'What did you do then?' To which Hopeful replied, 'What? Why I could not tell what to do.'

'Had you thoughts of leaving off praying?' Christian asked. 'Yes, an hundred times twice told,' Hopeful responded. 'And what was the reason you did not?' Christian asked him. 'I believed that that was true which had been told me,' came the response.' So Hopeful continued to pray until God gave him the answer of full assurance of salvation which he was seeking.'

Martin heard many things which were new to him. The possibility, for instance, that God may not immediately answer the prayer of some who seek pardon. And that he might delay in answering the request of believers in order to sanctify them further. How inconsistent such words at first seemed with the doctrine of conversion and evangelistic methodology that Tom Martin had been taught, yet how true to the biblical revelation of the sovereignty of grace. He says, 'One of the most precious memories I have of my own father is of the tears of joy welling up in his eyes as he left a church in Quarryville, Pennsylvania, after hearing Reisinger expounding the theme that saving knowledge of Jesus Christ is all of grace, from the words of Jesus to Peter recorded in Matthew 16:16, "Flesh and blood has not revealed this to you but my Father which is in heaven."'

Will Metzger has spent over thirty-five years working for the Inter-Varsity Christian Fellowship at a State University in Delaware. He is the author of a splendid book on evangelism *Tell the Truth* (IVP). He and I actually met in 1961 when we commenced our studies at Westminster Seminary in Philadelphia, and lived in Machen Hall for three years. Will was a freshman in Dickinson College in 1957, and he recalled in a letter to Ernie the personal interest he took in him:

'I had visited Grace Baptist Church, but wasn't quite sure what to make of it. It was the first time this young believer had ever encountered strong doctrinal preaching. I also had not been aware of Calvinism. I almost 'bounced off' this hard truth. Fortunately you drew alongside me and personalized these truths by showing how they drove you to evangelism and prayer. You demonstrated the *implications* of these great doctrines for piety and witnessing. Most of all you challenged my way of thinking and gave me time to react and question. I didn't feel pushed to make up my mind right away. You gave me books and showed me Scripture. You spent time with me. Your humor and confidence in the Holy Spirit to convince me helped me to come to my own conclusions.

'Some specific incidents which I remember are: a weekly letter sent from your office to me and another student containing our Bible Study for that week; invitations to 'go have a steak' with you and spending the time talking about Scripture; a day in the woods at Jake's Cabin reading through the book of Acts in order to find the marks of the church; recounting of incidents from your week of witnessing to your barber, a professor at the College and a golf partner. Your enthusiasm rubbed off. Your excitement for doctrine and solid Christian books was contagious.'

So those years were characterized by persistent wise student evangelism. It entailed giving to young men and women such books as Gaussen's *Inspiration of Holy Scripture*, E. J. Young's *Thy Word is Truth*, J. I. Packer's *Fundamentalism and the Word of God*, *Evangelism and the Sovereignty of God*, and *Knowing God*, Arthur Pink's *The Sovereignty of God*, Martyn Lloyd-Jones' *Studies in the Sermon on the Mount*, Iain Murray's *The Forgotten Spurgeon*, Thomas Watson's *The Ten Commandments*, and John Bunyan's *Pilgrim's Progress*. Such a ministry had an impact on many, particularly on the Inter-Varsity Christian Fellowship at Dickinson College. Among the students to be influenced by this combination of hospitality and literature were Walter Chantry and his wife Joie; Don Legget and Linda (the former a seminary teacher for many years in Canada); Andy Hoffecker (a professor at Reformed Seminary, Jackson, Mississippi); Penny Mitchell (a missionary translator with Wycliffe Bible Translators); Russ Sasser (a missionary to Indians in the jungles of Brazil, and later a pastor in Florida); Charles Fitzpatrick (a graduate of Westminster Seminary and a minister), and Janie Neuber (later the wife of Jim Eshelman, the first U.S. Manager of the Banner of Truth).

Janie Neuber started as a student at Dickinson in 1957 along with Will Metzger and was converted in her first year. Ernie sold her some books for a dollar each. He reckoned that books which had actually been purchased were more likely to be read than those which a student had been given *gratis* – unless the student could not afford one dollar! So students learned a valuable lesson about the danger of being a book 'collector' rather than a book 'reader'. Janie bought *Studies in the Sermon on the Mount* and *Thy Word is Truth* and over the following years such books as Packer's *Evangelism and the Sovereignty of God*. After she met Jim she gave him *Pilgrim's Progress* and Loraine Boettner's *Reformed Doctrine of Predestination*.

Once students gained a taste for books and truth they commended them to others. Tom Martin was given two of J. I. Packer's books by Walter Chantry. The president of the IVCF loaned him John Owen's *Death of Death* so that he might read J. I. Packer's Introduction, and he promised Tom that he would give him his own copies if he first read the loaned ones. Talking with others about Christian books in Grace Baptist Church basement became Tom Martin's informal seminary.

Tom himself was instrumental in helping fellow students Sue and Jim Taylor to see the truth. Sue was raised in a religious home but with little awareness of theology. She once asked her Methodist pastor if the Bible did not seem to support something called predestination. His response was quite perplexing to her: 'It certainly seems like that, doesn't it?' he muttered. When she arrived at Dickinson College in Carlisle she naturally gravitated to the Inter-Varsity Christian Fellowship where soon she heard of the doctrines of grace. She says:

'I blush now at the lame arguments I offered Ernie against election, or the laments Will Metzger had to endure about predestination. I was wrestling with putting a vital, experiential, sometimes charismatic life of belief under the scrutiny and authority of the whole of Scripture. It was a high view of Scripture, and the gentle persuasion of Tom Martin, that God finally used to break my stiff-neckedness. He took time to sit me down and look at Romans 3 and Christ as actual propitiation, and I was caught. How could I ever suggest that my Saviour's death could be ineffectual? I walked back to the dorm that night, continuing the futile argument with God and with myself until I finally gave in. I remember shaking my fist at God and feeling a literal crack in my spirit as I said, "I give up. It's there in Scripture, and I'll believe it; but I don't like it!" Since that time I've grown to love the doctrines of grace. They're my only hope, and they're the hope for a broken world, incapable of its own redemption.'

Jim Taylor, Sue's husband, left Carlisle for medical school and Ernie lost track of him until years later when the Reisingers moved to live in Cape Coral, Florida. Ernie asked a Presbyterian minister if he could recommend a family doctor. The preacher was pleased to suggest one of his own elders, a certain Dr Jim Taylor. Fifteen hundred miles from Carlisle, Pennsylvania, the Taylors were rediscovered, involved in their local church, with Sue a key person in Providence Christian School in Cape Coral.

During the early 1960s the literature ministry of the church took off. Grace Baptist's book table ministry began to purchase select titles from Baker Book House, Eerdmans Publishing Company, Presbyterian & Reformed, Reiner Publications, Sovereign Grace Publishers, Zondervan Publishers and others. Katie Irwin tended the church book room, located in the basement of the church. In one year $10,000 worth of Christian books were sold. Around the tables people could linger after the evening service and see the latest titles. The Wengers, the Irwins and others in the congregation were generous in giving away books, but none so much as Reisinger. He developed the widest literature ministry to students, preachers and missionaries, as well as the people to whom he was witnessing. 'Do the little things', he would say to fellow members, 'Be friendly to your waitress, give her a tract, bring a Bible to her little boy, write a note to a new college graduate, enclose some Christian literature; give books and books and books.' Ernie has made a lifetime of that work.

The church conceived of a ministry that would provide the best of books to other congregations for their own book tables. The publisher for which they were most enthusiastic was the Banner of Truth Trust which displayed the same love of experiential Calvinism as they did. On 21 January 1964 Ernie wrote his first letter to Iain Murray. He asked advice on a particular issue:

'I am writing for some guidance concerning a discussion in our local church (independent Calvinist Baptist). We all seem to lean to the Presbyterian idea of elders and deacons and yet we do not go so far as to outrule all local autonomy. My reason for writing is to inquire, is there some book or article or source of information that you could recommend that may be helpful. What I'm trying to say is this. We are a congregation of Baptists that is almost Presbyterian. We do not see a strictly congregational rule and yet we do not see the extreme hierarchy type of government. Would be grateful for any suggestion or help you may have.'

The enquirer little realized then that he was raising an issue which was to trouble Baptists in independent churches for the rest of the century.

In August 1966 Humphrey Mildred, the Banner of Truth's assistant manager from London, visited Carlisle to find out what was happening in this small town that had caused more Banner of Truth books to be sold there than anywhere else outside the British Isles. In December 1966, Ernie came on his first visit to the U.K. Iain Murray took him to the places where C. H. Spurgeon spent his early life, but Ernie was more interested in conversation than in places associated with church history. As they stood at Isaac Watts's grave in the Bunhill Fields cemetery, Iain Murray recollects that Ernie asked the attendant who had led them to the tomb if he knew Isaac Watts' God. The highlight of the visit was attending the Puritan Conference at Westminster Chapel, hearing such men as Paul Cook speaking on 'Finney on Revival', J. I. Packer on 'John Owen on Communication from God' and Dr Lloyd-Jones on 'Henry Jacob and the First Congregational Church'.

The following year Ernie spoke at the Leicester Conference and a few months later the two Banner trustees, Jack Cullum and Iain Murray, visited Carlisle. After these visits, with discussion and correspondence, Carlisle eventually became the centre of the Banner of Truth operation in America. During the past decades almost ten million Banner books and booklets have been sold, with the U.S. office responsible for 45% of that total.

For several years Ernie was the sounding board for book promotion in the States, providing day-to-day direction for the employees at the Carlisle office. On many occasions wise counsels were given to Jim Eshelman, who was to manage the American operation for over thirty years. Jim had left a lucrative career as an electrical engineer to do this work.

In 1968 the Banner of Truth recognized the worth of Ernie by inviting him to become their first American trustee.[1] When Ernie accepted the invitation, Iain Murray explained to him the articles of faith in the Trust deed:

'While the vexed point of baptism is not mentioned in the Articles of Faith, the Trust deed confirms that if any of these articles goes into dispute their interpretation is to be governed by the Westminster Confession and John Calvin's *Institutes* . . . If in the future the Trust passed under the control of militant paedo-baptists they could justify emphasis on paedo-baptism by asserting that it is implied in the Articles of Faith . . . If that time ever came it would be with the loss of your gifts and leadership, for obviously you would not be happy in such a set-up, and even more seriously it would mean the loss of good will from Baptists generally. However, I thought we ought to mention this point so that you know that the Trust deed is not strictly neutral on the point of baptism, but you have our assurance – an assurance which we wanted to make concrete by your becoming a Trustee – that the interdenominational policy we have followed these past ten years is the one we mean to continue' (personal letter, 22 November 1968).

[1] Ernie has cherished his connection with the Banner of Truth and has expressed warm appreciation of the contributions made over the years by his fellow-Trustees and by Mervyn Barter, Jim Eshelman, Humphrey Mildred and John J. Murray.

Neither Ernie nor the present author, both having worked with the Banner of Truth for many years, has felt any sense of marginalization because we are Baptists.

Books from other publishers are also now mailed out all over America from Carlisle through the agency of the Cumberland Valley Bible Book Service. Its founder, Fred Huebner, first met Ernie at a Christian and Missionary Alliance Church in North Caldwell, New Jersey, in 1964. Ernie gave him a bound copy of D. M. McIntyre's *The Hidden Life of Prayer*. At a conference in Carlisle in 1968 Ernie was responsible for Fred Huebner getting two big boxes of books from the Banner of Truth. *The Works of John Owen* became particularly cherished volumes.

Ernie's love of books and desire to distribute them to the masses as God directed him affected Fred Huebner. During a pastorate in the Mohawk Valley Bible Church in Herkimer, New York, Fred started the Mohawk Valley Bible Book Service with Ernie's encouragement and with the help of Banner of Truth and the Presbyterian & Reformed Publishing Company. It became clear to Fred Huebner that God had a different plan for him than the pulpit ministry. 'Trust in the Lord. Seek his direction,' urged Reisinger. Through some testing providences, Fred came to Carlisle to sell books that promoted experiential Calvinism world-wide and, from $250,000 of books sold in the first year, the sales are now approaching $2 million per annum. Fred Huebner says, 'So much of what happened in this movement can be traced back to Ernie and his prayerful distribution of materials. I can't begin to list the many men who have told me how they were introduced to the doctrines of grace because of the books Ernie gave them.'

12

THE LAST DECADE AT CARLISLE

WALTER J. CHANTRY WAS RAISED IN PHILADELPHIA. His father worked for the FBI and Walter went to the famous Germantown High School from which at graduation he moved to Carlisle to study in Dickinson College. It was during his first year at the College in 1956 that the church changed its name from Grace Chapel to Grace Baptist Church. Henceforth the fellowship intended to subscribe to the 1689 London Baptist Confession of Faith. Walter Chantry had had a nominal Presbyterian background but was drawn increasingly into the life and witness of this congregation. He received his Christian moorings and doctrinal roots through his contact with the ministry and membership of the church. Anthony Cunio was then the pastor, while Walter served as president of the Inter-Varsity Christian Fellowship at Dickinson. Both he and his wife-to-be Joie benefited from Ernie's discipling. If Ernie were to speak at a Christian Business Men's Committee meeting in Pennsylvania he would take Walter along with him. As they drove they would discuss the teaching of the Bible. Walter would join in prayer for Ernie's ministry that evening, and then, on the way back home, there would be more spiritual discussion. He would return to College with a book, tract or tape for further instruction. When Walter wrote his first book, *Today's Gospel,* he dedicated it thus:

'There are three men who have been of considerable help to me in producing this book. I would like gratefully to acknowledge their kind labour and counsel. They are: A carpenter, who has been my spiritual father and principal teacher in the faith; A merchant, who has faithfully shared the oversight of our local church throughout my brief ministry; An Arab, whose love for Christ and spiritual fellowship has immensely enlarged the joy of my sojourn.'

There is no need to guess the identity of the 'carpenter.' In 1958 Walter's father died aged 43. On 7 March Ernie wrote to him:

'It was only this morning that I learned of your present grief, but so it pleased the Lord, whose will must be our will, if we would be happy. I am sorry that I never knew your dear father, however, in some measure I do feel that I knew him, and it is hard to believe that he has gone to be with the Lord at this early age.

'May His grace be sufficient for such an hour as this. As sorrow cuts like a knife at a tender spot so may the reality of this occasion ever be real and vivid to your own heart as you face the duties and responsibilities of life. What must it be like to face times like this for those who have no hope in the Gospel of our Lord Jesus Christ? Take time to thank him for the Balm of Gilead.

'As the Lord reminds me I will remember you at the throne of grace and your dear ones as they face the painful reality of laying aside your dear father. May Jesus be real to you.

Sincerely yours, in Christ's love and care,

Ernest C. Reisinger.'

In the spring of 1959 Reisinger proposed to Walter (then still at Dickinson) that the two of them labour together to begin a church in a community near Carlisle called Shiremanstown, under the oversight and with the permission of Grace Baptist Church. A few months later Walter moved to Shiremanstown where he and Ernie surveyed housing districts in the community and made personal contacts with unchurched people. They rented the Ranchland Dance Hall for Sunday services.

Throughout the next year Walt taught the Sunday School hour, Joie played the piano and Ernie preached in the worship service. God was pleased to bring together a congregation and after a year Grace Baptist Church purchased a house in Shiremanstown remodelling it as a place of worship. A few months later an experienced pastor was called to oversee the work. Ernie encouraged more church planting projects in the state in Mechanicsburg, Paradise, Hazelton and Chambersburg.

Such outreach was based upon preaching the Word of God, but it was not founded on sermons exclusively. The apostle Paul reminded the elders in Ephesus that he had preached publicly but also from house to house. One of Ernie's great gifts was his ability to come right alongside people, and witness to those whom God had brought into his life. One example of this is seen in his dealings with one of the poorest men of Carlisle. When Ernie left his morning prayer meetings with Roger Irwin and drove to his office he regularly passed an old man pushing a broken-down cart with two wheels. His job was to pick up rubbish placed at the back of several restaurants and push the cart to the town dump. He used much of the money he earned to buy cheap wine. Ernie had noticed this man and, coming straight from his prayer meeting with Roger, his frequent sights of the pathetic figure made him more sensitive to the man's lostness.

It was on an autumn day that Ernie first stopped his car and offered the man a ride. He got into the car with Ernie and, needing a handkerchief, received one of Ernie's own. The man's name was Jim Camron, and he perked up at this unexpected kindness, thinking that Ernie might also give him some money. Instead he heard about the love of God in Jesus Christ and the eternal life he would enjoy if he turned from his sin and trusted the Lord.

About two days after that meeting Ernie noticed in the local paper that Jim Camron had been admitted to hospital, a motorist having hit him and broken his leg. Ernie started to visit him. On the second occasion he gave Jim a shave, and talked to him again about the Lord Jesus. On a subsequent visit Ernie noticed another man sharing the little ward. As he entered the room the man called him across to his bed and asked whether he were a Christian. When he said 'Yes', the man replied, 'So am I, and I am trying to get out of this room. I have asked the nurses and the doctors. I want to get away from this fellow. He swears, and he curses, and he . . .' Ernie cut him short: 'Too bad,' he said, 'God put a mission field at the foot of your bed and you want to get away from it.'

Though the churches at Carlisle, Shiremanstown, Mechanicsburg and Chambersburg had public preaching as the climactic heart of their worship, they also fostered a loving and faithful spirit of personal testimony resulting from an overflow of devotion to Christ. The belief prevailed that pulpit witness without individuals evangelizing would have been hypocrisy. A prayer meeting had to fire compassionate involvement in the hearts of the people praying or intercession would prove an unavailing religious exercise. One did not ask

God to do what one was too lazy or afraid of doing oneself. One prayed for strength to do one's duty.

At the Carlisle church a schoolgirl invited a friend to the services and after some time she became a true Christian. She began attending the prayer meetings, and one night when the pastor asked if there were any requests for prayer she said, 'Pray for my Daddy. He's not a Christian.' There were a number of occasions when she reminded the church not to forget her father. A natural opportunity arose for Ernie to visit the man when he was in hospital, but as Ernie talked to the sick man about the claims of the Saviour he looked up at him and said, 'I never did anything wrong.' That terminated the conversation.

Then one night at the prayer meeting the girl herself prayed, speaking of a number of concerns, until she got to the theme of her father's lostness. Then she broke down and wept. After that there was a pause before anyone else felt they could pray. Ernie was reminded of the apostle Paul's references to his tears: 'Serving the Lord with all humility, with many tears and trials which happened to me by the plotting of the Jews' (*Acts* 20:19), and again, 'Therefore watch, and remember that for three years I did not cease to warn everyone night and day with tears' (*Acts* 20:31). Referring to this incident at their morning prayer meetings, Ernie told Roger, 'I believe that God is going to do something for her father.' He remembered Elmer Albright's grief over his own sustained resistance to the gospel.

One Sunday when a Christian businessman was staying with Ernie, the young people from the church drifted along to the Reisingers' home in the afternoon as was their custom. So the businessman began to talk to them one by one asking about their families, and whether they were from Christian homes or not. He was getting nearer to this teenage girl and Ernie knew that this theme would be a sensitive area to her. 'What does your father do?' he asked her. He worked in the post office. 'Is he a Christian?' Her face flushed and tears ran down her cheeks. She buried her face in her hands. Her questioner looked down, and then he slid along to Ernie's side of his seat and looked at Ernie. The body language said it all: 'We must go to that man right now.' Ernie looked at his watch. It was an hour before the evening service. There were many reasons to plead the inconvenience of the hour, and Ernie's faith was weak, even though he had said to Roger that he thought God was going to do something for that man. Ernie remembered the man's words at the hospital, 'I never did anything wrong', and his hostility to anyone talking more to him about religion. These thoughts inclined Ernie to remain where he was and go straight to the service, but his friend kept looking at him with anticipation. 'You want us to visit her father?' 'Yes', he said. So they got up, went to the car and drove to his house on their way to church.

Ernie recounts what happened:

'When the doorbell rang, the father came to the door. He knew me from the previous visit and invited us in. Sure enough, they had company, and the mechanical baby-sitter was on full blast. My friend is a stockbroker and they have a great deal of diplomacy. In the construction business, we do not have much of that. So, I went over to the television and said, 'Dad, we've come to talk to you about something important. You don't mind if we turn off the TV, do you?' He turned it off. My friend did the talking. He told this man some things about Christ. Then he told him what had happened in my home that afternoon. Then I saw that man change. Humbled, he finally got down on his knees and cried to God for mercy.

That same man who once said to me, "I never did anything wrong", that Sunday afternoon called out to God for mercy.'

The beginning of that change of life was a burden on the heart of a teenage girl which she innocently passed to the whole church, and together they longed and worked for that man to know God for himself. Although the Carlisle church grew through the preaching of the Word of God it was necessarily accompanied by personal testimony to the reality of Christ, and earnest prayer for those who heard the gospel. 'It is a sin to preach and not to pray', Ernie often says.

During the last decade of his involvement in the construction business (he retired in 1966 at 47 years of age) Reisinger was not only an elder in Grace Baptist Church, involved in church planting in Shiremanstown and Mechanicsburg, and committed to the Christian Business Men's Committee Meetings, he was also involved in starting ministers' conferences in the eastern U.S.A. Through these conferences Associations of Reformed Baptists came into being. Family Conferences also resulted as a spin-off of this activity. Today they are a part of the Christian landscape of America and beyond. There are at least eight annual Reformed Baptist conferences in various parts of the U.S.A. and others in Great Britain, Canada and South Africa. Ernie was also speaking in meetings all over the U.S.A. about once a month. Wherever he preached he also spoke personally to people and subsequently sent them literature.

In the mid-1960s Ernie was taking a youth conference at a ski retreat in the mountains of Connecticut. After driving all day through ice and snow to reach the ski resort, he decided to spend the first evening simply outlining the course of the week's studies. He told the group that they would be examining the marks of the second birth as set forth in the First

Epistle of John. After the evening session ended he retired to his cabin to rest, but found his peace interrupted when several of the leaders knocked on his door and insisted on coming in and speaking to him. The first question out of the box was whether he knew a man called Al Martin. Ernie had never heard of him. They explained to him that Al Martin had been their conference speaker the previous year and he had had the same emphases in his messages as Ernie was intending to bring to them. Ernie noticed that they seemed pleased that he was covering those kinds of topics. The time there was a blessed occasion, but Ernie could not get this man out of his mind. There were not many he knew to be speaking on these themes.

After the conference was over, Ernie went back to Carlisle via New Jersey where Al Martin was then pastoring a Christian and Missionary Alliance church. They immediately struck up a friendship, there being just a fifteen-year gap in their ages. Ernie was able to help Al Martin in a number of ways and especially in his theological quest. He had come to believe in the Bible's teaching on election, but he was struggling with the question of whether the Scripture actually taught particular redemption. Their conversations built up a little heat, so that Al made Ernie promise not to raise the subject of limited atonement again. Ernie was happy to do so but he gave Al Martin a copy of John Murray's *Redemption – Accomplished and Applied* with the words, 'If this book doesn't help you see the truth of particular redemption then go on being what you are, and keep preaching what you are preaching.' Some time later, he invited Al and his wife to accompany him to a conference in Kentucky to hear Dr Martyn Lloyd-Jones preach. During the trip Al's wife took Ernie aside and told him that if he wanted to bring up the subject of particular redemption again Al wouldn't object. From studying the Bible he had come to embrace the belief that Christ had died in order effectually to save all those multitudes of God's own chosen people.

For many years there was a close esteem between the two men. On 19 July 1973, Al Martin wrote to Ernie in response to a recent telephone call:

'I want to express to you, my dear brother, my heartfelt thanks for all your loving counsel, your gracious exhortations through the years, and above all, for your faithful prayers on my behalf. I count it one of life's greatest blessings that my gracious God has surrounded me with friends like yourself, who love me enough to rebuke me, to admonish me, and to instruct me in order that I might know my Saviour better and serve him more efficiently . . . You can see what is upon my heart. If I were to receive the news today that the Lord had taken you home to be with Himself, these are some of the things that I would no doubt wish I had said while you were here. Hence, since you are here, I have said them and feel release in my spirit. It was a delight to see you even for a few hours last week, and I trust that God will enable us to spend some time together before too long.

Affectionately in the bonds of Christ, Al.'

In 1963 Ernie had some influence over a former Church of the Nazarene student who was considering entering the Southern Baptist denomination. His name was R. T. Kendall. Fourteen years later he was to follow Glyn Owen as the minister at Westminster Chapel, London. Ernie was visiting the Thirteenth Street Baptist Church in Ashland, Kentucky to hear the elderly evangelist Rolfe Barnard preach. The congregation were singing this hymn of John Newton's:

In evil long I took delight,
 Unawed by shame or fear,
Till a new object struck my sight,
 And stopped my wild career.

I saw One hanging on a tree,
 In agonies and blood,
Who fixed his languid eyes on me,
 As near his cross I stood.

Sure never till my latest breath
 Can I forget that look;
It seemed to charge me with his death,
 Though not a word he spoke.

My conscience felt and owned the guilt,
 And plunged me in despair;
I saw my sins his blood had spilt,
 And helped to nail him there.

A second look He gave, which said,
 'I freely all forgive;
This blood is for thy ransom paid;
 I die that thou may'st live.'

R. T. Kendall, who was sitting behind Ernie, had never seen the hymn before that service and, noticing how moved Ernie had been by the words, he leaned across and said to him, 'That's enough to set you on fire, isn't it?' They met briefly after the service and Kendall thought that they would never meet again, but during the following week some books sent by Ernie arrived at his home, including Dr Martyn Lloyd-Jones's

Studies in the Sermon on the Mount. He immediately began to read it and was gripped by it, writing opposite the title page, 'What I have read in this book has had a greater singular influence on me than any other book I can think of. I am particularly grateful for chapters 17–21. This book crossing my path has been one of the outstanding events of my life. It came to me when I needed it the most.' A few weeks later Kendall heard Dr Lloyd-Jones speak at the Winona Lake Conference in Indiana.

R. T. Kendall proceeded to write a Master's thesis at the University of Louisville on 'The Rise and Demise of Calvinism in the Southern Baptist Convention'. He sent a copy to Ernie, who was fascinated by the evidence of the Southern Baptist Convention actually having Calvinistic roots. Ernie returned the favour by sending to R. T. Kendall the complete works of John Calvin and John Owen.

But as the years passed the men did not continue to enjoy theological harmony. As Kendall says, 'When I made the distinction between Calvin and the Puritans with particular reference to the Atonement and the doctrine of Assurance, Ernie was extremely disappointed in me. I have to say that this caused a bit of estrangement in our relationship, but I am indebted to him beyond words. I only know that I thank God with all my heart for his influence over me.'

A Reisinger family group. Back row, left to right: Sarah (grandmother), Ernest Gilbert (father), Howard (grandfather). Front row, left to right: Arthur and John (uncles).

Cordelia Weller Forney Reisinger (mother).

Ernest aged sixteen.

Mother, Ernest and Donald (son), 17 September 1944.

At the beginnings of Reisinger Bros., Ernest in October 1946.

Ernest leading a Bible Class at Biddle Mission, Carlisle, 1947.

Brothers and sister with father: Back row – Ernest and Donald; Front row – Grace, Father and John.

Ordination service at Mechanicsburg, 17 October 1971, with Cornelius Van Til.

Left: Ernest and Mima Jane Reisinger, after the Leicester Conference, 1973.

Right: Martyn and Bethan Lloyd-Jones. 'One of the greatest men that I have ever met and one of my mentors. When we were together at the Niagara Falls on one occasion, I was hopeful of pursuing theological discussion but he seemed strangely disinterested, and then declared, "I do not believe you have a single aesthetic bone in your body!"'

Left, top: Mervyn T. Barter, General Manager of the Banner of Truth, 1972–99.

Right, top: Ernest with Walter J. Chantry, Pastor of Grace Baptist Church, Carlisle, in 1985.

Bottom: James B. Eshelman, Banner Manager at Carlisle, 1967–2001. 'These three friends have all been a vital part of my life, two as colleagues in the work of the Banner of Truth Trust.'

Top: With James I. Packer, December 1980. 'Another friend and mentor whose writings have meant so much to many.'

Bottom: With Mima Jane in the late 1990s. 'After Jane had suffered a stroke, a one-mile walk from our home in Cape Coral became our daily routine.'

'Three good friends of mine from Pompano Beach. They would often be with me for a time before the hour for morning school.'

13

WESTMINSTER THEOLOGICAL SEMINARY

In 1965 Ernest Reisinger was considering his future. Within a year he was to retire from the construction business, handing it over to his son Donald, and then the Reisingers might even leave their beloved Pennsylvania to live in a warmer part of America. To prepare for the upcoming changes he tendered his resignation as a deacon at Grace Baptist Church. Having held that office since 1952 he had become convinced that his church attendance had become too infrequent for responsible office-holding. His church-planting evangelism each Sunday morning and his participation in laymen's crusades sponsored by the CBMC caused him to miss many services. He wrote a warm letter of appreciation to the church, mentioning each deacon by name and speaking of his genuine affection for each of those officers. Then on 31 December 1965 he ceased to be a deacon of Grace Baptist Church, Carlisle, a congregation which owed its origin under God more to him than to any other person.

The following year Ernie retired from Reisinger Brothers, Inc. to devote the next twelve months to promoting the work of Westminster Theological Seminary, Philadelphia. That may come as a surprise to some people, but it indicates how his reputation had spread far beyond the confines of his home town. He felt able to accept the Seminary's invitation to be involved in this enterprise because of his years of experience working with students at Dickinson College, and through the influence God had given to him in encouraging young men to embrace the whole counsel of God. Ernie also had an unusual measure of the grace of exhortation by which he lifted men to being better pastors, and gave to traditional Reformed denominations a new taste of a heritage some were taking for granted.

It may be wise to set Westminster in its historical context. Just over thirty-five years earlier, in 1929, Princeton Theological Seminary in New Jersey was reorganized. The General Assembly of the Presbyterian Church in the U.S.A. which controlled the seminary abolished its Board of Directors, placing it under a nominated single Board of Trustees. Its president, Dr J. Ross Stevenson, a moderate in a generation of moderates, wished to make the seminary representative of the varied schools of theological thought within the Presbyterian Church in the U.S.A. He had worked for fifteen years to attain that goal and eventually succeeded, so the days of Princeton Seminary as a conservative school were numbered.

As a consequence some members of the faculty decided not to teach any longer at Princeton, but to join in the founding of a new seminary in the city of Philadelphia to be named Westminster Theological Seminary. Its first classes were held at 1528 Pine Street, a residence belonging to Dr Oswald T. Allis. With fine generosity, he offered it to the Seminary for its classes. The rent was to be one dollar a year, though it is doubtful if it was ever paid. It opened its doors only a month before the Wall Street crash on Black Thursday, but without any debts, thanks in part to Dr Machen's own generosity. A few years later the seminary moved to a large detached house in landscaped grounds in Glenside, a township eighteen miles north of centre-city Philadelphia, not far from the Pennsylvania Turnpike. That is where it remains to this day. So 'Princeton' had moved much nearer to Carlisle.

From Princeton's faculty came the brilliant gifts and scholarship of men such as Robert Dick Wilson, J. Gresham Machen, O. T. Allis and Cornelius Van Til. R. B. Kuiper also joined the faculty. The Scotsman John Murray came a year later. In due course they were joined by some of their most able and devout students, Edward J. Young, Ned B. Stonehouse, Paul Woolley and Edmund P. Clowney. There was also an incomparable librarian named Arthur Kuschke. They all loved Machen and everything that he stood for. After the departure of O. T. Allis from Westminster's staff, Machen's premature death in 1937, and the flight of the fundamentalists led by Carl McIntire to open a rival seminary, this team of men refused to panic. They settled in to train men for the ministry of the Word according to their own light and power and their commitment to the Westminster Confession of Faith.

This they continued to do throughout the lean war years of the 1940s when student enrolment was very small. The Seminary required of entering students a liberal education to bachelor's degree level, and to them it presented the old Princeton theological curriculum. The text book in Systematic Theology employed by John Murray was Charles Hodge's three volumes. Machen's own superb Greek grammar continued to be the text book used for the next fifty years. The staff never lost courage, nor their warm regard for one another.

At this Seminary at the end of the fifties newly-married Walter Chantry arrived. He had grown to appreciate both the life of Dr Gresham Machen and his denomination, the Orthodox Presbyterian Church. Its leaders (who were not from one ethnic group like the Dutchmen of the Christian Reformed Church) had done much to preserve the witness to historic Christianity in twentieth-century America. At the Seminary Walter was instructed by the godliness and wisdom of such men as John Murray, Cornelius Van Til and Edward J. Young. At this seminary in 1961, I met Walt Chantry, and also, in the fall of 1963, Ernest Reisinger himself when he was invited to speak to its students at a Fall retreat at Quarryville. At those meetings all the students received from Ernie a copy of Horatius Bonar's *Words to Winners of Souls*.

In May 1965 Reisinger visited the Seminary to hear Dr J. I. Packer speak at a Ministers' Institute. He called at the office of one of the administrators named Robert den Dulk, and that day a mutually-enriching friendship began which continues to the present. The following Monday was a holiday, and Bob den Dulk and his family spent the day in Carlisle with Ernie and Duke Irwin. Ernie had a cabin in Perry County, near Carlisle, a place to rest and be nourished. It had a fine little library for the convenience of its guests. That cabin became the den Dulks' second home for fourteen years. Over time it was to be the place where as a family they would build some values that they would not trade for anything in the world.

At the 1964 graduation from Westminster Theological Seminary the students scattered. I returned to Wales, while Bob den Dulk was invited to join the Seminary's administrative staff. It was his growing friendship with Ernie which helped clarify some of Bob's thinking about the ministry and the influence a seminary might have upon its students. These were some of his conclusions:

'I realize only God can prepare a man's heart for ministry, but I speak of this in the context of what are the things that happen at seminary that will have an impact on a person's life as he goes out to preach the Gospel. Surveying the life of a professor has as much an impact as does the actual teaching which goes on in the classroom. I have often reflected upon the hours spent in Ernie's study, or at the cabin, or on his patio, where we talked together, poured out our hearts to God in prayer and sought to sharpen one another. Those are the kind of things that form a man's ministry. Ernie's thoughts had an influence on the shaping of Westminster Seminary in California when I was appointed its second president. I thank God today for the way professors have a heart for the pastoral ministry and can be spiritual mentors to the students who go there. It was Ernie who helped me to think that way.'

Especially within Bob den Dulk's own family, Ernie was a true counsellor and friend. When relations between Bob and his father Gilbert were strained, Ernie's help was invaluable. In 1971 he flew to California to seek a healing between father and son. Gilbert had severed his relations with his other son Clarence whom Bob greatly loved. In 1983 Ernie flew out to bring reconciliation once again, but Gilbert refused to attend a meeting which Ernie had set up. All this was a painful learning experience for Bob, but in every struggle God was teaching him lessons. How thankful he is today that his relations with his own sons are so different from those he knew with his father. Bob den Dulk would be the first to acknowledge that that is all through God's free grace.

Through the encouragement of Bob den Dulk, and with the active support of Edmund P. Clowney, the newly-appointed

President of Westminster Seminary, Ernie was invited in 1966 to promote the seminary across the U.S.A. Ed Clowney set up an itinerary from Maine, in the north-east of America, to the very south of the continent in Miami, Florida, and then westwards to California. This year of travel gave Ernie a more mature understanding of the state of American Reformed churches.

After each trip Ernie would present a report to President Clowney, and soon a pattern of concerns emerged. The churches believed that the seminary was turning out too few preachers, and that its graduates were weak in evangelism. In other words, graduates of Westminster had forgotten that the truth they had learned was truth *for people*. They were not asking what effect their teaching of the Bible was having, through the Holy Spirit, on the lives of those listening to them, both Christians and unbelievers. They knew about the history of the church, and they knew about Old Testament and New Testament times. They knew accented Greek from Machen's *Grammar*, and also Hebrew from a manual authored by E. J. Young himself. They had been taught theology by John Murray, presuppositionalist apologetics by Cornelius Van Til, and exegesis and principles of the history of redemption by everyone. No one in the congregations could teach these young men anything in such theological disciplines. When it was suggested that their competence was not as satisfying to the congregation as they imagined, they could become defensive. Personal spirituality was an area that needed to be taken more seriously than many did.

Ernie began his work in January 1966 by visiting Robert Atwell, then the minister of Galloway Orthodox Presbyterian Church in Miami. Atwell himself had also spent some time in promoting the seminary amongst the churches and at a few colleges. He was considered to be one of the most experiential and evangelistic graduates of Westminster Seminary. Atwell described to Edmund Clowney the effects of Ernie's visit to his congregation:

'I thought that the Tuesday evening meeting was clearly blessed by our God. Coie brought down eighteen men and we had twenty-four of our men out but, of all the other men I'd invited and all the promises I had, there were just twelve who came. However, the fifty-four seemed to fill one side of the church and it looked like a good crowd. Ernie was superlative. I'm fully convinced that Westminster couldn't possibly have a better man representing the institution. What I mean is that a better job of representing the Seminary couldn't be done by anyone. Ernie is quite persuaded that having a meeting of a more or less public nature at which he can speak to interested men is the way to provide a quick opportunity to talk subsequently to individual men on an informal basis. I'm sure it is one good way. What I want especially to say, however, is that I am persuaded that he will do a job of real value to the Kingdom and to the Seminary wherever he goes and whatever the circumstances. I'm sure that will be increasingly true as he makes additional trips and has a backlog of acquaintances . . . I do think that he should be given every encouragement to continue his work. That he is not cocksure of himself is an added bonus. I haven't been as inclined for some years to praise the Lord for the situation at Westminster as I am now with your attitude and the prospect of having Ernie working with you.'

The message Ernie brought to these gatherings promoting the seminary had several strands. There was firstly his commitment to historic Christian doctrine. He would warn his hearers that the congregation that neglects to teach sound biblical doctrine weakens the whole church membership. It works against true unity. It invites instability in its fellowship, lessens conviction and stalemates true progress in the church. When Ernie spoke of 'doctrine' he was always referring to foundational truths, those that were set forth, defined and defended at the Synod of Dort in 1618, and later expressed in the Westminster Confession and also the Baptist Confession of 1689.

Those confessions set forth a God who saves, not a little God who just tries to help man to save himself. Those doctrines reveal the three great actions of the Trinity for the recovering of poor, helpless, lost men, that is, election by the Father, redemption by the Son and calling by the Spirit. All of these are directed to the same individuals and infallibly secure their salvation. Such teachings give all the glory of saving sinners to God and do not divide it between God and sinner. Those doctrines see the Creator as the source and the end of everything both in nature and in grace. Those doctrines say history is nothing less that the working out of God's pre-ordained plan.

They set forth the God who is sovereign in creation, sovereign in redemption (both in planning and perfecting it), sovereign in providence, and sovereign on the contemporary scene, that is, sovereign right now. Those doctrines set forth a Redeemer who actually redeems, a God who saves by purpose and by power, the Trinity working together for this end – the salvation of sinners. The Father plans it, the Son achieves it and the Holy Spirit communicates and effectually applies it to God's elect. Those doctrines set forth a God who saves, keeps, justifies, sanctifies, and glorifies sinners, and loses none in the process. God saves sinners! Men must not weaken this great truth that God does save them by trying to disrupt the unity of the work of the Trinity, or by dividing the achievement of salvation between God and man. Jonah sets it straight in Jonah 2:9, 'Salvation [past, present and future] is of the LORD.'

To emphasize these great truths incidentally helped to establish Reisinger's own credentials as a Baptist who held to the great doctrines of the Reformation. Most of the supporters of Westminster Seminary were Presbyterians, while some were members of the Christian Reformed Church, but most of them had never heard of Reformed Baptists, or even knew that such people existed. But more importantly it also served to assure them that these truths were still taught and loved at Westminster Seminary. Ernie presented these doctrines in such a fresh way that they found their hearts were kindled anew in love for them. Having heard them from childhood, many Presbyterians considered them a little old- fashioned, whereas Ernie spoke of them like a man who had dug a hole in a field and stumbled across wonderful treasure.

Another strand to his teaching was that Christian experience emerges from doctrine. Christian experience is the influence of sound biblical teaching applied by the Holy Spirit to the mind, the affections, and the will. True religion is not some mystical, nebulous feeling, floating around in the sky. It cannot be anything less than right thinking in respect to God, right feeling in respect to the Bible and right acting in respect to God's will. Therefore true religion must reach the whole man. It must reach his mind because that is what he thinks with; it must reach his affections because that is what he feels with, and it must reach his will because that is what he decides with.

To maintain this right thinking, feeling and acting in respect of God three things, Ernie would say, are needed: a quiet place, a quiet hour and a quiet heart. Consider Paul's deep hunger expressed in Philippians 3:10: 'That I may know him and the power of his resurrection, and the fellowship of his sufferings, being made conformable to his death.' The doctrine Paul believed created a deep personal hunger for Christlikeness. The Shulamite's testimony is too frequently true of ministers and other Christian workers, 'They made me keeper of the vineyards, but my own vineyard I have not kept' (*Song of Solomon* 1:6)

Nor can there be true Christian experience without self-denial. Self-denial is not eradicating one's own sin by a crisis experience, but rather a life that foregoes lawful liberties. Though the Reformed churches emphasized 'Christian liberty', Ernie reminded them that the following four principles must always guide the Christian who exercises his freedom:

1. *The Fear of God.* As the servant of Christ, he must act out of the motive of love to God, and all objects must be used for God's glory. The term 'liberty' is often used as a cloak for malicious self-indulgence, which is sin.

2. *Love of the Brethren.* Though no man may dictate to a Christian's conscience, the welfare of fellow saints must always deeply affect his decisions. In a spirit of serving the brethren he must do that which he judges will edify them and prevent their stumbling.

3. *Watchfulness over the Soul.* Though the believer is free in conscience to use all of God's creation, carefulness in practice is demanded of him because of remaining lusts. Where the Christian judges himself weak through lust, he must abstain for the sake of perseverance.

4. *Compassion for Sinners.* Use of liberty must always be regulated by its effect upon sinners, and that behaviour chosen which is likely to win some.

Whatever experience chills our fervour, dissipates our mind, diverts our attention, or occupies an inordinate proportion of our time or interest is the right eye that we are called to pluck out and cast from us.

The third strand in Ernie's messages was the importance of evangelism. He often bore witness to the life of Elmer Albright and his faithful words to himself. Elmer had taken Christ seriously when he said, 'You are witnesses of these things' (*Luke* 24:48), and 'You shall be witnesses unto me' (*Acts* 1:8), and 'Go into all the world' (*Mark* 16:15). Elmer had a world. It was not Africa, China, South America or India. It was a construction world and Ernie was in that world. On the human side Ernie became a Christian because God sent a true witness across his path who was not ashamed of Jesus. He knew that the gospel was his trust.

God had entrusted the awesome task of evangelization to clay instruments, even human messengers. The story of the gospel is the story of one man telling another man of Christ, and of that man telling yet another, and so on down through all history. That certainly is not the whole story, for God must do his sovereign work. But on the human side, there is not a Christian anywhere who cannot trace his conversion back to the prayers and faithful witness of a godly father, or a godly mother, or pastor, or teacher, or friend, or church. If we could take a chain from our lips to the man who told us, and the one who told him, and so on, we could chain all our testimonies to the lips of Jesus Christ himself when he said, 'Go into all the world and preach the gospel.' Thank God that his followers are still obeying him. True witnessing is nothing but an overflow of devotion to Christ.

As the year ended, Bob den Dulk wrote a message of appreciation to him from the Seminary: 'I want to express my deepest appreciation for everything you have done for the Seminary in the past year. There are some lives which have begun to show some fruit, some students who have begun to see some of the glorious truths of the doctrines of grace. You have been an inspiration to us all and your godliness both in doctrine and life is something for us all to strive for. And please don't misunderstand me. I'm not saying anything that I don't mean from the bottom of my heart. I love you too much as a brother for that. Your influence is particularly felt because you are a layman, not a professor or minister and you have no axe to grind. The financial blessings have been tremendous as well. We thank God for the support you have given and for the amount you have stimulated.'

When Ernie spoke for the cause of Westminster Seminary near Ripon, California he was the guest of Dr Gilbert den Dulk. This meeting resulted in the establishment of the den Dulk Christian Foundation. It began as a trust to support Reformed theological education, spread Reformed truth to churches and Christians outside the Reformed community by using doctrinally sound literature, and contribute to missions and evangelism by translation work, publishing and helping needy students and missionaries. Amongst its directors today are James Adams of Cornerstone Church, Mesa, Arizona, Andrew Anema of Visalia, California, Bob den Dulk's sons Gilbert and Timothy, and Dr Robert Godfrey, president of Westminster Seminary in California. Ernest Reisinger is chairman of the board and Bob den Dulk is president.

The June 1984 den Dulk Foundation annual meeting was an important occasion when its future goals were clarified under the direction of Ernie Reisinger. Since that time it has persevered with clear goals. For example, it has given grants to Westminster Seminary, the Westminster Conference in

London, Banner of Truth conferences, and the National University for Evangelicals in the Dominican Republic. It has helped underwrite the reprinting of such volumes as the *Abstract of Systematic Theology* by James P. Boyce, the *Works* of Herman Witsius, and Fairbairn's *The Revelation of Law in Scripture*. Some of these books have been printed and distributed for the Foundation by the Presbyterian and Reformed Publishing Company. The Banner of Truth Trust has helped in translating into Spanish such books as Ernie's own *Today's Evangelism*. The Foundation has distributed volumes to Master of Divinity students at Westminster Seminary in California and Westminster Seminary in Philadelphia, Mid-America Reformed Seminary, Reformed Seminary in Orlando, Jackson, and Charlotte, Covenant Seminary, and Calvin Seminary. It has distributed free books to many pastors in Third World countries especially to hundreds of preachers in Peru.

The Foundation carries on a thriving prison ministry through the part-time services of a retired prison chaplain who places Christian books in all fifty-one prisons in the state of California. Plans are also being made to take the prison ministry beyond California. Inmates have been furnished with New Geneva Study Bibles at subsidized prices. The Russian translation of the New Geneva Study Bible has also been made available in study centres established by the *Christ for Russia* organisation. A major project of providing an annual volume of sermons in Spanish has also been undertaken.

Ernest Reisinger's involvement in the den Dulk Foundation was one of the most fruitful consequnces of that year which he spent promoting Westminster Theological Seminary, back in the 1960s.

14

ORDINATION IN MECHANICSBURG, PENNSYLVANIA

As already noted, Ernest Reisinger retired from the construction business in 1966 at forty-seven years of age. After the first year dedicated to promoting Westminster Theological Seminary, Philadelphia, he and Mima moved to Plantation Key, Florida. At first the change was to avoid the freezing winters of Pennsylvania, the climate of Florida being much kinder to Ernie's respiratory problems. Summers were spent at the home which they kept in Carlisle. There were also preaching missions almost monthly all over North America, and occasional visits further afield, to Jamaica, and to Leicester, England, where he spoke along with Eric Alexander at the Ministers' Conference of the Banner of Truth in 1969 on the theme, 'The Spiritual Needs of our Time'.

He also was persuaded to pay a visit to Switzerland for the European Workers' Conference of Child Evangelism Fellowship. Its European leadership wanted to encourage biblical evangelism to be practised amongst their workers. For twenty-nine years Sam Doherty was full-time European Regional

Director and since his retirement he has written a dozen fine books on children's evangelism. At this Conference seven different languages were spoken, with almost as many people translating Ernie's ten messages on evangelism. He made some good friendships with the British workers, and was to enter into correspondence with Kenneth Martin of the Irish CEF. At one time Martin wrote, 'I have just finished reading your book *Today's Evangelism*. Time after time my heart warmed to what you had to say. How I wish all evangelicals and especially those involved in evangelism would take time to read such a book as yours . . . We in European CEF continue to press on with our desire to improve our methods in evangelism and the contents of the children's Bible lessons.'

Then in the winter of 1969, Grace Baptist Church in Carlisle called on Ernie to help them with some difficulties which had arisen in their mission church in Mechanicsburg, Pennsylvania. There was no one they could think of as suitable as himself to pastor that congregation for a short time and put it on a stable foundation again. It was not easy to think of leaving the warmth of Florida for the north, but Ernie and Mima believed that it would be for about a year. That was not to be the case. There were hints of some problems arising in the Reisinger Brothers, Inc. construction business, as well as in the dairy farms, and suddenly also in his family. But these were still on the horizon, and Ernie was drawn initially back north by the teething troubles of this new Reformed Baptist congregation with its strong personalities and their convictions. Yet by returning to Pennsylvania his skills as a pastor and expositor were tested and strengthened, and he became secure in his calling to the work of the gospel ministry.

It was at this time he reached the conclusion that he needed to be officially recognized as a man summoned by God to be a preacher, and so formally ordained. His gift of expounding and proclaiming the Word had long been recognized by the Carlisle congregation. After two years pastoring the Mechanicsburg church, Ernie came to a conviction that being set apart to the work of the gospel was God's will for him. His fiftieth birthday came at the beginning of this period in Mechanicsburg and the solemn sense of having received a high calling to the work of the ministry would not leave him.

So in mid-October 1971 elders from the Carlisle church and other Reformed Baptist churches in the area gathered with the leaders of the Mechanicsburg congregation to examine Ernie concerning his fitness for the work of the pastor-preacher. It was not a merely formal examination, though he was older than many of them and they were all indebted to him in different ways. They sat with him and asked him such earnest questions as these:

'Do you believe the Scriptures of the Old and New Testaments to be the Word of God, the only infallible rule of faith and practice? Do you sincerely receive and adopt the London Confession of Faith of 1689 which this church upholds as containing the system of doctrine taught in the Holy Scriptures? Do you promise subjection to your brethren in the Lord? Have you been induced, as far as you know your own heart, to seek the office of the holy ministry from love to God and a sincere desire to promote his glory in the gospel of his Son? Do you promise to be zealous and faithful in maintaining the truths of the gospel, and the purity and peace of the church, whatever opposition may arise against you on that account? Do you engage to be faithful and diligent in the exercise of all private and personal duties which become you as a Christian and a minister of the gospel, as well as in all relative duties and the public duties of your office, endeavouring to adorn the profession of the gospel by your conversation, and walking with exemplary piety before the flock over which God shall make you overseer? Are you now willing to take the charge of this congregation, agreeably to your declaration when you accepted their call? And do you promise to discharge the duties of a pastor there as God shall give you strength?'

Then, after answering the following questions, he was installed as the pastor:

1. Are you now willing to take charge of this congregation as its pastor, agreeably to your declaration when you accepted its call?
2. Do you conscientiously believe and declare, as far as you know your own heart, that in taking upon you this charge, you are influenced by a sincere desire to promote the glory of God and the good of his church?
3. Do you solemnly promise that, by the assistance of the grace of God, you will endeavour faithfully to discharge all the duties of a pastor in this congregation, and will be careful to maintain a deportment in all respects becoming a minister of the gospel of Christ?

The members of the Mechanicsburg church were then asked:

1. Do you, the people of this congregation, continue to profess your readiness to receive Ernest C. Reisinger, whom you have called to be your minister?
2. Do you promise to receive the word of truth from his mouth with meekness and love, and to submit to him in the due exercise of discipline?
3. Do you promise to encourage him in the arduous labour and to assist his endeavours for your instruction and spiritual edification?

4. And do you engage to continue to him, while he is your pastor, that competent worldly maintenance which you have promised, and whatever else you may see needful for the honour of religion and his comfort among you?

On 17 October 1971 the public services of recognition were held in Mechanicsburg. His brother, John Reisinger, preached the charge to Ernest, and Dr Cornelius Van Til of Westminster Theological Seminary preached the charge to the congregation. Anyone frequenting Westminster Seminary for a year or more came under the influence of Dr Van Til, and grew to love and respect this man of God. His combination of freshness defending the faith, formidable intellect, domestic happiness and winsome piety was irresistible. When the first volume of Arnold Dallimore's *Life of George Whitefield* appeared Van Til was spotted mowing his lawn with the book in his hand. Ernie loved him, as did all who came to know him.

Reaction to Reisinger's ordination from the churches was overwhelmingly positive. Al Martin was glad that Ernie's gifts were recognized for what they were – those of a true preacher – and that he would no longer have the luxury in pastors' conferences of giving messages from the perspective of the pew addressing the pulpit. Instead he would have to acknowledge the humbling role of being himself a preacher standing in a pulpit just like the rest of his ministerial brethren. That was a fair comment. The act of ordination certainly recognized Ernie's call to exhort men and women to serve the Lord with more zeal. The laying on of the elders' hands gave him nothing more than what God had already bestowed upon him.

Yet others were unsure of the rightness of this step. R. T. Kendall, the future pastor of Westminster Chapel, London, was one of those who were uncertain of the wisdom of the step. He wrote: 'Ernie and I used to have a difference of opinion as to whether he should be ordained a minister. I felt his letting people ordain him was a mistake. When I first knew him he was a layman – a very powerful and erudite layman at that. He knew more theology than most ministers, but when he became a minister, he was in a sense like the rest of them – even if he were a cut above them. I thought his influence was far more vast as a layman than as a minister, but he had to do what God led him to do.'

It was for Ernie a simple recognition of God's leading over the previous thirty years, and a preparation for the fruitful future which would extend over a further thirty years of Christian work, with about half of these spent in pastoral charges. Thus years of great influence lay before him. He could not have stayed permanently in this preacher/non-preacher no-man's-land. He had spoken about 'lay-preaching' to Dr Martyn Lloyd-Jones in 1963 on the latter's visit to the U.S.A. Dr. Lloyd-Jones was not over-excited about such activities. When in 1968 Ernie heard of his ill health he had written to the Doctor to sympathize, and this theme of 'lay-preaching' was again raised in the letter:

May 20, 1968.

Dear Doctor,

Some time ago I learned of your being laid aside and have recently heard you are progressing speedily toward recovery. I thank God for this.

I felt this morning I wanted to just drop you a few lines telling you how greatly God has used you in my own life and in the lives of many, many men in this country. Time would not permit me to recount the number of testimonies of preachers as to the great help they have received from your writings, and when I meet the men from your country, such as Jim Packer,

Iain Murray and others, they have personally acknowledged to me their deep love and gratitude to God for your life and ministry. They have both called you 'father' in the proper sense of that expression.

I enjoyed a brief visit with Jim Packer when he was in this country recently. We discussed ecclesiastical separation in a very candid manner, even though our views are quite opposite. I feel if he would see this it would be the means of making a great man greater, however, I am not God and must leave the servant with his Master.

I have been very busy 'lay-preaching'. I have a vivid recollection of your comments on lay-preaching and I am glad you allowed for an exception in the case of Howell Harris! I have not sought these requests and invitations – mostly Presbyterian.

I have been corresponding somewhat with Mr Dallimore on his important work on that great giant, Whitefield. I am so anxious for this work, and plan to do my best to promote it. Your encouragement has meant a great deal to him.

By the way, if you ever learn of another portrait of Whitefield similar to the one you have, I would appreciate knowing about it.

If there is a chance of your coming to the U.S. my wife and I would be delighted to entertain you and your dear lady.

My wife joins me in sending greetings to you and your wonderful help-meet.

Affectionately in Christ, E. Reisinger.

Dr Martyn Lloyd-Jones wrote a number of letters to Ernie over the years. In one letter he had said, 'We must keep in touch at all costs in these days of confusion and transition.' He further wrote to Ernie:

28 May 1968

My dear Friend,

How very kind of you to write to me. Nothing has more greatly helped and encouraged me during the past months than to know that good friends like yourself have been thinking of me and praying for me.

I am delighted to let you know that I am making very rapid progress and beginning to feel myself again and already looking forward to resuming work in September.

I have also heard from Mr Dallimore and am glad that he is really getting on with this important work. As long as it is out in time for the celebration of the bicentenary of Whitefield's death in 1970, all will be well.

I am glad of your various activities and am sure that God will bless you greatly. I hope you are well as a family.

My wife joins with me in sending much love to you both,

Yours very sincerely, D. M. Lloyd-Jones

Ernest Reisinger thus took up the work of pastoring the Mechanicsburg congregation, and establishing and settling it took the next three years. In this period he was privileged to baptize thirteen people. There were twenty-five additions to the membership. In fact the first six months after his ordination was one of the most blessed periods of ministry of his life. It was after that that he had to climb Hill Difficulty and enter upon a most trying and depressing time. In June 1972, less than a year after his ordination, pressures compelled him, in addition to maintaining the Mechanicsburg pastorate, to take over his floundering Reisinger Brothers construction business again and work hard to keep it from going under.

It was in those troubled days that Bob den Dulk and his family determined to visit Mechanicsburg to hear their dear friend preaching. Matters were coming to a head concerning the construction company and Ernie's growing conviction was that it should be sold, and the dairy business too. There was a sense of weariness with the business world which he had been a part of for so long. Ernie was now anxious to be out of it, even at some loss. He had shared some of these things with Bob (whose brother Clarence was eventually to purchase the farms and herds) and that August Sunday night, as the den Dulk family sat in the congregation, they heard a sermon they would never forget. Writing years later to him about that message Bob den Dulk said:

'It is an evening that is as clear in my mind as if it were yesterday. In the sermon you made reference to the graveyard outside the church and you asked the question, "What would you prefer to have on your tombstone, that you owned the greatest cows in the world, or that you preached Christ and him crucified?" At that time you actually did own some of the greatest cows in the world. Your ultimate decision was to preach Christ and Him crucified.'

By the end of the year Ernie made up his mind to resign from the Mechanicsburg church. It was now on a firm foundation and they needed another leader. He felt that, because of the close relationship of many in the congregation to his business, its general geographic location, and his business problems, it was wise and necessary for him to relinquish his responsibilities there. Some men in the church sought to dissuade him from resigning and insisted that he stay, but the strain was too much. Ernie tendered his resignation and he and Mima returned to live in Florida.

15

CHILDREN

During the 1970s, when Ernest Reisinger had become a full-time minister of the gospel, his first funeral service happened to be that of a three-year-old girl. He cried to God, 'What shall I say or preach at this funeral to give comfort and hope to this young couple and their relatives?' His thoughts turned to these words in the Gospels,

'And they brought young children to him, that he should touch them: and his disciples rebuked those that brought them. But when Jesus saw it, he was much displeased, and said unto them, Suffer the little children to come unto me, and forbid them not: for of such is the kingdom of God. Verily I say unto you, Whosoever shall not receive the kingdom of God as a little child, he shall not enter therein. And he took them up in his arms, put his hands upon them, and blesssed them' (*Mark* 10:13–16).

First, Ernie pointed out how Jesus rebuked those who kept little children from coming to him. Second, he showed how the Lord Jesus expressed his love for them by taking them up in his arms. Thirdly, Christ blessed them, 'for of such is the kingdom of God'. Ernie then consoled the grieving family by pointing out that Christ's present attitude in heaven is surely not less than he demonstrated on earth. When another young couple lost their little boy in a fatal accident he encouraged them with that same warm sympathy, adding, 'I feel some of your pain and grief.'

It was John Bunyan's approach to children that encouraged Ernie not to forget them. From Part Two of *Pilgrim's Progress* the twenty-first century church can learn the simplicity and relevance of catechizing our children:

'And because *Prudence* would see how *Christiana* had brought up her children, she asked leave of her to catechise them: So she gave her free consent. Then she began at the youngest, whose name was *James*.

Prudence. And she said, Come *James,* canst thou tell me who made thee?

James. God, the Father, God the Son, and God the Holy Ghost.

Prudence. Good boy. And canst thou tell who saves thee?

James. God, the Father, God the Son, and God the Holy Ghost.

Prudence. Good boy still. But how doth God the Father save thee?

James. By his grace.

Prudence. How does God the Son save thee?

James. By his Righteousness, Death, and Blood and Life.

Prudence. And how doth God the Holy Ghost save thee?

James. By his Illumination, by his Renovation, and by his Preservation.

Then said *Prudence* to *Christiana,* You are to be commended for thus bringing up your children. I suppose I need not ask the rest these questions, since the youngest of them can answer them so well. I will therefore now apply myself to the next to youngest.

Prudence. Then she said, Come *Joseph,* will you let me catechise you?

Joseph. With all my heart.

Prudence. What is man?

Joseph. A reasonable Creature, made so by God, as my brother has said.

Prudence. What is supposed by this word *saved?*

Joseph. That man, by sin, has brought himself into a state of captivity and misery.

Prudence. What is supposed by his being saved by the Trinity?

Joseph. That sin is so great and mighty a tyrant, that none can pull us out of its clutches but God; and that God is so good and loving to man as to pull him indeed out of this miserable state.

Prudence. What is God's design in saving of poor men?

Joseph. The glorifying of his Name, of his grace, and justice, and the everlasting happiness of his creature.

Prudence. Who are they that must be saved?

Joseph. Those that accept of his salvation.

Prudence. Good boy, *Joseph,* thy mother has taught thee well, and thou hast hearkened to what she has said unto thee.

Then said *Prudence* to *Samuel,* are you willing that I should catechise you also?

Samuel. Yes, if you please.

Prudence. What is Heaven?

Samuel. A place and a state most blessed, because God dwelleth there.

Prudence. What is Hell?

Samuel. A place and state most woeful, because it is the dwelling place of sin, the Devil, and death.

Prudence. Why wouldst thou go to Heaven?

Samuel. That I may see God, and serve him without weariness; that I may see Christ, and love him everlastingly; that I may have that fulness of the Holy Spirit in me; that I can by no means here enjoy.

Prudence. A very good boy, also, and one that has learned well.

Then she addressed herself to the eldest, whose name was *Matthew;* and she said to him, Come, *Matthew,* shall I also catechise you?

Matthew. With a very good will.

Prudence. I ask then, if there was ever anything that had a Being antecedent to, or before God?

Matthew. No. For God is eternal; nor is there any thing, excepting Himself that had a being, until the beginning of the first day. *For in six days the Lord made heaven and earth, the sea, and all that in them is.*

Prudence. What do you think of the Bible?

Matthew. It is the Holy Word of God.

Prudence. Is there nothing written therein, but what you understand?

Matthew. Yes, a great deal.

Prudence. What do you do when you meet with places therein that you do not understand?

Matthew. I think God is wiser than I. I pray also that he will please to let me know all therein that he knows will be for my good.

Prudence. How believe you as touching the Resurrection of the Dead?

Matthew. I believe they shall rise, the same that was buried; the same in *nature,* though not in corruption. And I believe this upon a double account. *First,* because God has promised it. *Secondly,* because he is able to perform it.

Then said *Prudence* to the boys, You must still hearken to your Mother, for she can learn you more. You must also diligently give ear to what good talk you shall hear from others; for your sakes do they speak good things. Observe also, and that with carefulness, what the heavens and the earth do teach you; but especially be much in the meditation of that Book that was the cause of your Father's becoming a Pilgrim. I, for my part, my children, will teach you what I can while you are here, and shall be glad if you will ask me questions that are godly and edifying.'

So Ernest Reisinger has time for children, and they trust him. He shows them affection, and never belittles them. If he is also able to help them in practical ways he does, as this letter indicates:

19 May 1960

Dear Uncle Ernie,

You are a kind uncle to send me to camp for a week and I would like to thank you very much. I am looking forward to going, and will tell you all about it when I get back.

Love, Cordelia Ann Lins.

2 September 1969

Dear Mr Reisinger,

Thank you for helping to send me to the Christian school. I enjoy going there and like having Devotions in the morning, and the references to the Bible during classes, Mr Rhine's teaching, and his telling of his travels in other lands. I also enjoy the textbooks and being together like a one-room schoolhouse. I know that you care about me and my soul. Only by God's help am I trying to obey Him.

Love, Peggy.

Conversations he has with children may bear lasting fruit:

22 December1975

Dear Mr Reisinger,

I am writing to tell you that I was baptized last night. I am very happy. A lady named Mrs Lewis was baptized also. I have wanted to be a Christian for a long time and I'm thankful that the Lord gave me that desire. Then for a long time I wasn't sure whether or not I was a Christian. But now I have assurance that God saved me. Romans 10:9 has helped me: 'That if thou shalt confess with thy mouth the Lord Jesus, and shalt believe in thine heart that God hath raised him from the dead, thou shalt be saved.' That helped me because I do believe, and when I talked with Mr Wenger and went before the elders and was baptized I was confessing with my mouth. Also the book by Gardiner Spring, *The Distinguishing Traits of Christian Character* has helped me. I'm not far in it but I found certain traits in me such as love to God, repentance for sin, and faith in Christ. I have always remembered when you talked with me at Harvey Cedars. That has helped me a lot and I wanted to write to you since I was baptized because I thought you might like to know.

There isn't much else to say, so goodbye.

Love, Judy Chantry.

Others have written letters to him after he has spoken in the church they are attending, and he has happily corresponded with them:

November 1984

Dear Brother Reisinger,

I really have enjoyed your sermons. If it wasn't for you there would be fightings in my house. I hope you will pray for me and my family. You have really helped me. I think you are really nice. I have not been saved yet, but I will soon. Well, I have to leave now as its almost time for church. If you can write to me that would be good. Here is my address,

Love, Hiram Walker.

Ernie replied to Hiram:

My dear young friend,

I very much appreciated your note, and I was very glad that you know the state of your soul. You said you were not saved. That is the second best state to be in. Why do I say that? Let me explain. The best state to be in is to know that you are saved with a well-grounded biblical assurance. The second best state is to know that you are not saved. Why? Because you are likely to become a diligent seeker. The worst and most dangerous state is those who are self-deceived.

The first step in coming to this state is to be truly convinced of sin. This is the work of the Holy Spirit and his first work upon your soul. The world says you are an innocent and harmless boy. Do not believe them. The world is a liar. Pray to see yourself exactly as God sees you that you may joyfully receive the Lord Jesus Christ who obeyed God perfectly, and died for sinners. May you forsake all and follow Jesus Christ. You are welcome this day to stand righteous before God in Jesus.

Grace be with you!

Your friend in Christ,

Pastor Ernest C. Reisinger.

P.S. Please give my Christian greetings to your mother.

December 1984

Dear Pastor Reisinger,

I finally get to write to you. How are you doing? I am doing good. Mom got me a new Bible. It is a King James version. It has red letters. It has my name on it written in gold. And it is black. I got baptized Sunday night.

In my new Bible I am reading Luke 1:5-80. So far it is good. Mom and Dad are OK. Thanks for the letter! Have a merry Christmas! I wish you were still here. I miss you!

Grace be with you!

Your friend Hiram.

January 1985

Dear Hiram,

Thank you for your letter. It was nice of you to write, especially the good news about openly confessing Christ in baptism. I am enclosing a couple of little books that will be very helpful to you, *God Made Them Great*, and *Pictorial Pilgrim's Progress*. The Christian life gives inward peace and joy that the world cannot give. However, at the same time, it is a life of warfare against our inward temptations and outward temptations.

I am enclosing a little poem that expresses this struggle and warfare. It is by a great preacher and hymn writer, John Newton. He wrote the hymn that I like to call our Baptist Anthem, 'Amazing Grace'. This little note comes with my warm Christian love and greetings to you and your family,

Your friend in Christ,

Ernest C. Reisinger, Pastor.

Dear Brother Reisinger,

How are you doing? I am doing fine. Thank you for the letter, and for the books. And the poem. I am reading *Pictorial*

Pilgrim's Progress. You shouldn't have bought them for me. I was sick the day I got your letter. It sure made me feel good.

Love, Hiram,

P.S. Give my greetings to your family.

Dear Bro. Reisinger,

I would like to thank you very much for the special attention you have shown to my son Hiram. Your letters, phone calls, and books have meant a great deal to him and me. He has already read *Pilgrim's Progress* and has loaned it to a friend.

So many things in our family have changed for the better since your meetings in our church. I know this is a result of the Holy Spirit working. My husband has not missed a Sunday morning service in two months. This is the first time this has happened in the sixteen years we have been married. I am praying that he, too, will soon be baptized.

Thanks again for your kind concern.

Your sister in Christ,

Edna Walker.

17 January 1985

Dear Hiram,

Thank you for your little note, and please thank your mother for her note also.

Hiram, since you liked *Pictorial Pilgrim's Progress* you should also have the real *Pilgrim's Progress*. Next to the Bible I think *Pilgrim's Progress* is one of the five most valuable books I have ever read. I have read it eighteen times and get new Biblical insight each time I read it. Charles Haddon Spurgeon, probably the greatest Baptist preacher that ever lived, read it a hundred times. I am also enclosing a brief biography, *The Beggar's Bible* about another great man. I think you will enjoy reading it.

Please give my warm Christian greetings to Pastor Tullock and your family (*Prov*. 3:1–8).

Your friend in Christ,
Ernest C. Reisinger,
Pastor.

22 April 1985

Dear Hiram,

I really do appreciate getting the little notes from you. The Lord brings you and your family to mind quite often. I wish we could be closer together. I am so glad that you have a true pastor that believes and practises the Bible.

I am enclosing a little book for you about Martin Luther, *A Child's Life of Luther*. I hope you enjoy it. Let me know when you finish it and I will send you something else.

With warmest Christian love and greetings to you and your family.

Your friend in Christ,
Ernest C. Reisinger
Pastor.

Ernie writes to Christian George, the son of Timothy George, the Dean of Beeson Divinity School in Birmingham, Alabama.

30 July 1993

Dear Christian,

When I saw this new edition of *Pilgrim's Progress* and the fine art work I thought of you because of your name, Christian. There are lots of pictures of Christian on his way to the Celestial City. I hope you will like it. John Bunyan is my 'patron saint'! I have read that book many times and I learn something new each time I read it. Bunyan has unusual insight into the Christian life, both its joys and trials.

Give my warm Christian love and greetings to your parents and Alyce.

Your friend,
Ernest C.Reisinger.

Dear Dr Ernest Reisinger,

Thanks a bunch for the *Pilgrim's Progress* you gave me. It's well written. I know that you are sick and need people's prayer. Well, every night (or almost every night) we pray for you. Tonight we are going to especially pray for you to get well. I have 5 copies of *Pilgrim's Progress*, including the one you gave me. Timothy George and Denise George (my mom and my dad) give you greetings. We pray that you will get better, but if you don't; like in *Pilgrim's Progress*, every Christian will go to heaven.

Hope you get well soon,
Christian George.

9 November 1993

Dear Little Pilgrim,

Thanks so much for your letter. It was most encouraging.

Your father told me you are collecting editions of *Pilgrim's Progress* from around the world. You have chosen a big assignment. *Pilgrim's Progress* stands next to the Bible in sales and translations. It has been translated into 198 languages. There are 50 editions in Africa alone.

We did a real search before selecting the volume I am sending to you, under separate cover. The paper is good, the binding is good and the text is good. Don't neglect the second part of Bunyan's book. That is where you will find the children (the second generation Christians). I like it better than the first part, if that is possible!

This comes with warm Christian greetings to your mother, your father, and your little sister.

Mercy, peace and love be multiplied to you and yours,

Ernest C. Reisinger.

Dear Brother Ernie,

Greetings, my friend, in the Name of our Lord! I trust that this letter finds you in improving health and good spirits. We really missed you at the Founders Conference here in Birmingham this summer. You must take heart at the good influence for the work of the Lord which you have had on so many younger ministers of the gospel, among whom I am pleased to count myself one.

Thank you so much for the letter and books which you sent to Christian. Denise joins me in sending our affectionate regards to both you and sister Reisinger.

Yours in the bonds of grace,

Timothy George,

1 June 1990

To Joe Nettles, Illinois.

My dear friend Joe,

Congratulations on completing your High School education. I pray that you will always remember the grand object of your education, that is, that it contributes to the glory of God who gave you your existence, talents and gifts. On Him, also, you are dependent for their preservation. It is most reasonable, therefore, that these powers, gifts and talents should be empowered to His service for ever. I am enclosing a little gift for your graduation present.

You will soon be leaving the influence of a Christian home and godly parents; therefore, you will face new temptations and dangers. May our Lord be pleased to help, guide and protect you.

Joe, the most important counsel I could give you, or any young Christian man, is this, never to make an intimate friend of anyone who is not a friend of your God. I do not mean that you have nothing to do with anyone but true Christians, but be very careful in your choice of friends. Ask the question, Will this friendship benefit my spiritual life? Follow the example of David who said, 'I am a companion of all them that fear thee, and of them that keep thy precepts' (*Psa.* 119:63).

May our Father in heaven keep you safe from all harm, give you diligence in your studies and fortitude, wisdom in all your decisions, integrity in your living and a Christ-like example to others.

Your old friend,

Ernest C. Reisinger.

P.S. Try hard to find a good church to attend.

* * * * *

Parents are exhorted by Ernie to bring up their children to know the Lord. He urges them not to strive with their children. Be gentle. Teach them. Forbear with them. Do it in meekness. Correct them. Children need to be evangelized and are capable of knowing God for themselves. The means is teaching the Holy Scriptures to them, accompanied by prayer and biblical discipline. Ernie loves this poem of Robert Murray M'Cheyne:

Children Called to Christ

Like mist on the mountains, like ships on the sea,
So swiftly the years of our pilgrimage flee;
In the grave of our father how soon we shall lie!
Dear children, today to a Saviour fly.

How sweet are the flowers in April and May!
But often the frost makes them wither away.
Like flowers you may fade: are you ready to die?
While 'yet there is room', to a Saviour fly.

When Samuel was young he first knew the Lord,
He slept in His smile and rejoiced in His word:
So most of God's children are early brought nigh:
Oh, seek him in youth – to a Saviour fly!

Do you ask me for pleasure? Then lean on His breast,
For there the sin-laden and weary find rest.
In the valley of death you will triumphing cry –
'If this be called dying, 'tis pleasant to die.'

16

A ONE-TIME PRODIGAL SON

DON REISINGER, ERNIE'S DELIGHTFUL ONLY CHILD, once wrote to his father, 'Although I am very thankful, be assured, that you are my father, it has not been easy to be the son of a great and strong man.' Don, with many responsibilities as President of Allen Dairy Farms, Inc., father of six children, a deacon in Grace Baptist Church, actually fell away from the faith. His marriage ended in divorce, and for years Don walked in a wilderness far from God, while Ernie and Mima ached for their prodigal. All the privileges of his home and the hearing of a biblical ministry each week no more kept him from falling than similar warnings and instruction prevented Peter denying his Lord.

Don was removed from the membership at Grace Baptist Church in Carlisle. For Ernie and Mima there were many tears and prolonged anguish of spirit. Such hard providences from God are a fiery furnace. It is not appropriate to draw back the curtain of these inner struggles any further than the principals involved will allow.

Donald's wife Patsy, behaved blamelessly through all those years, and remains a member in Grace Baptist Church today.

It meant a lot to her when many years later Don was calling her about the pregnancy of one of their daughters and then, after some time, he asked, 'Have I ever apologized to you for what I did?' Most of their children have come to confess Jesus as their Lord and Saviour and have married in Christ and are raising their children to love and serve him.

Concerning Ernie and Mima, there were a few characteristics they displayed through this trial which were public for all to see. Neither of them made the mistakes so common to parents in these circumstances:

1. There was never the least opposition to or irritation with the church when Donald was disciplined. They both believed deeply that all degrees of church discipline can be used by Christ in the day of the Lord (*1 Cor. 5:5*) as a means of saving the soul, so that the sinner is not condemned with the world (*1 Cor.* 11:32).

2. They never in the least blamed Don's wife for what had occurred. They remained as affectionate toward her and supportive of her as if they were her natural parents. Their sincere love for Patsy opened doors to the hearts of their grandchildren, particularly in their teenage years, which they used for the gospel of Christ.

3. Never did they lose faith that Don could be recovered, nor the hope that God could wipe away negative consequences in the lives of his family. Often they would say to people such things as, 'The story is not yet all told.' Their own faith in a wise, mighty and merciful God was never shaken.

Yet the trial was severe, as the following long letter to Don written by Ernie attests:

19 June 1973

My dear son,

It is 3:30 a.m. and again I am unable to sleep and, as many other nights lately, I either lie in bed or get up thinking and praying about you and the awful state you are in.

You obviously do not want to see me, your mother, or anyone who cares about your soul; therefore, I take up pen again, the third time, to write and plead with you to consider your state, practically and spiritually and eternally. Your desire to stay away from the people who are at least trying to do right in this world should, in itself, make you suspicious of your precarious condition. I had some hope the humiliation of being found out would bring repentance and mercy but it seems to have hardened you more.

You laughed a few months ago when I sent you the steps of Mr Temporary (the man who lived next door to one Mr Turnback) a vivid and perceptive picture by Mr Bunyan as to why and how men turn back. These steps should be no laughing matter now, and you should be able to identify them more vividly in your experience.

Let me review them with you: First, remember this backslider lived in a town about two miles away from 'Honesty', under the same roof as Mr Turnback. The man was much awakened once, he had some sight of his sins, and the wages of his sins. Well, why did he go back?

1. Though his conscience was awakened his mind was not changed; therefore, when the power of guilt wore away (which provoked him to be religious) he turns to his own course again even as a dog turns to his own vomit. He was hot for heaven only because of a sense and fear of hell.

2. Second, because of a slavish fear of men which became a snare (*Prov*. 29:25).

3. Third, to think and meditate on guilt and terror are grievous to the backslider. He does not like to see or think of his misery before he comes to it.

4. Fourth, the shame that attends true religion is a great block to the backslider.

Donnie, let me review what I then wrote to you as to *how* (the steps backward) and as I review them I plead with you to honestly apply them to your present case.

1. He draws off his thoughts, as much as he can, from the remembrance of God – Death and Judgement to come. This is secret – subtle – in his heart. And now grace becomes weak, sickly, ready to die.

2. He casts off (by degrees, of course) duties such as closet prayer, the curbing of his lusts, sorrow for sin. Oh, he may still go through the motions of outward religious activity and retain his judgement of truth but there is no enjoyment in it nor is he influenced by the truth anymore; in fact, sometimes these outward observances of religious activities may act as a lullaby to his sleepy soul and rock him to sleep, thus adding to his delusion. Bible reading becomes cold and formal, with no desire to know the mind of the Spirit in order to be obedient, holy and like Christ.

3. Then there is the shunning the company of lively and warm Christians. This makes way for the enjoyment of non-Christian company and the enjoyment of ungodly men.

4. This leads to coldness and indifference to public duty, such as hearing, reading the Word of God and holy conversation.

5. Then he begins to pick holes (find fault) in the coats of some of the godly and that devilishly; this means a seeming reason to throw religion and Christ behind his back. Yes, all the saints have holes in their profession but the worst of them

is not as wicked as the ungodly. Their sins are not the bent of their lives nor the desire of their hearts.

6. Then he begins not only to associate with but to adhere to loose and carnal men and women.

7. Then he gives way to carnal, wanton discourses, . . . bad movies, . . . reading in secret. And he is glad if he can see such things in any who profess true religion so that he may be more bold and do it through their example under the guise of Christian liberty – but still secretly.

8. Then he openly begins to play with sin.

9. Then he begins to be hardened and shows himself for what he has been inside and secretly.

Surely you can trace at least some of these steps.

Donnie, I have taken Bunyan's steps and changed the words by adding and subtracting but I have kept the principles of this wise and prudent saint. Let me sum up the causes for turning back: cares of the world – Luke 8:13–14; improper companions and connections; inattention to secret duties, prayer, etc; self conceit and dependence – 'I don't need God'; a wrong indulgence of legitimate things – playing with temptation.

Let me come now to what should seriously interest and concern you, that is, the consequences – very practical and certainly applicable to you this hour:

1. Loss of character.

2. Loss of comfort – satisfying your unchanged lust doesn't comfort very long at a time.

3. Loss of usefulness and power in Christ's church.

4. Loss of assurance.

5. You are and will, in a greater way, incur God's displeasure.

6. Your conscience is wounded and hardened.

7. You have scandalized others and given the enemies of

Christ and His church reason to laugh and scorn. Yes, you have filled their mouths with fuel to blaspheme God's truth and His people.

8. You have caused the faces of Christians to blush with shame and the weak to go into deep doubt and depression. See 2 Sam. 12:14 – David's case.

9. And now I want to emphasize the last consequence because you have not received the ripe fruit and terrible wages of this yet. You have only begun to see the fruit of this last consequence of turning back. That is this – bringing temporal judgement on yourself and your family. Psalm 39:31, 32 says, 'If they break my statutes and keep not my commandments; then I will visit their transgressions with the *rod* and their iniquity with stripes.' David's house is the shameful example of a temporary backslider: Incest – Amnon with Tamor; Murder, Absalom of Amnon; his own son warred against him; David knew no peace because the sword never departed from his house.

But there are also biblical examples of permanent backsliders. No better could be used than Saul and Judas. Won't you consider their end with me for your own good? Saul was anointed king – exalted to a high place. So were you, both in the church and in the community. I will not take the time to follow the details of Saul's life (I have already been writing for two hours. It is now 5:30 a.m.) but look with me toward the end itself. In 1 Sam. 26:21 we find these words of Saul: 'I have played the fool and have erred exceedingly.' And surely in 1 Sam. 28:35 these are some of the most pitiful and painful words in all the Bible, the words of Saul the apostate: 'I am sore distressed . . . God is departed from me, and answers me no more, neither by prophets nor by dreams.' And last in 1 Sam. 34:4 we see the end itself. The story of all apostasy. He took a sword 'and fell upon it'. Saul was not restored. For it is impossible for those who were once enlightened . . . if they shall fall away to renew them again to repentance. My dear son, an enlightened person has an infinitely, solemn responsibility. Judas' case is no different because in Matt. 27:5, after he was filled with his own ways and cast down the pieces of silver in the temple he departed and 'went out and hanged himself'. Prov. 14:14 says the backslider 'will be filled with his own ways'. Judas and all apostates will be 'filled with their own ways'.

Now, my dear son, I do not write these words to threaten you because neither I, nor any human being, knows at this point if you are a permanent or temporary backslider. Only God knows. But God in His wisdom and mercies does give us in his Word examples of both permanent and temporary cases which I prayerfully submit to you.

Oh, but I will not stop here because the worst thing that you can do is to think your state is irrecoverable or hopeless. The very opposite is true. Lost steps may be retraced. Grace may be restored, yes, and joy may fill your soul again.

Consider Samson's prayer. Samson's prayer contains two things. First, he prayed, 'Remember me.' Second, he prayed, 'Strengthen me.' Let me quote the words of this poor, adulterous weak man; I beg you to make them your own words: Judges 16:28 – 'And Samson called unto the Lord, and said, O Lord God remember me, I pray thee, strengthen me, I pray thee . . .' Pray for God to remember you and pray to God to STRENGTHEN you.

Alas for your father and mother, your wife and your children if there is no avenue of return. Alas for us if God our Father no longer welcomes the prodigal home. Alas for us if the blood of Jesus no longer heals a wounded spirit. Oh son, remember the truth of Scripture, there is a fountain that was open to the house of David for sin and uncleanness and it is not closed to sinning saints. Alas for us if the Holy Ghost no longer restores the lost joys of God's salvation.

May I assure you on the authority of God's truth and a broken heart that longs to see you spare yourself of temporal judgement and eternal punishment that there is a lingering affection in the heart of the Father, a welcome in the blood of Jesus and a restoring power in the operation of the Spirit for all returning backsliders.

Herod is suffering the judgement of God and the silence of Jesus, which is hell enough, not because he didn't hear the preacher (John the Baptist) or because he didn't obey many things the preacher said, but because he would not get rid of the woman that was unlawful for him to have. Mark 6:20: 'Herod feared John knowing that he was a just man, and an holy, and observed him and when he heard him, he did many things and heard him gladly' – But he would not get rid of the woman.

I pray that you are saying, 'But Dad, how?' I hope you are. In closing let me give you these suggestions:

Acquaint yourself with the real state of your soul before God. Seek to discover the cause of your failing (friends – how you spend your time – T.V. – movies, reading – whatever the cause might be). Take your case to the throne of Christ, His love for sinners, His love to sinners – His compassion – His promises. Set out anew for God and heaven on the narrow road, as though you had never started that way before.

Oh, how I wish paper and ink could carry feelings and not just words. Ah! but my hope and prayer is that God will do what paper, ink and words cannot do.

Time 7:30 a.m. A long letter: I know this is a long letter but it may be the last one I write to you – please, not only read it but try to feel it. Yes, it is a long letter and I pray God will reward my weak efforts for His name's sake and for the sake of your never-dying soul.

Your grieved and pained father.

Thus Ernie exhorted his son. The hymn-writer James Montgomery, who wrote such hymns as 'Hail to the Lord's anointed' and 'O Spirit of the living God', trudged through years of backsliding. Then he began to seek the peace he had lost and the God he had left. He wrote these verses at that time:

> I left the God of truth and light:
>   I left the God who gave me breath,
> To wander in the wilds of night,
>   And perish in the snares of death.
>
> Sweet was His service, and His yoke
>   Was light and easy to be borne;
> Though all His bands of love I broke,
>   And cast away His gifts with scorn.
>
> Lo, through the gloom of guilty fears,
>   My faith discerns a dawn of grace;
> The Sun of Righteousness appears
>   In Jesus' reconciling face.

After many years that Sun did rise again in Don's life, and a new day began. He was at last enabled to fall before Christ. Laden with a sense of his rebellious, self-willed past, his pride and ambition, he trusted that his Saviour of old would receive him back and restore him. He longed once again to belong to Christ utterly and only. His faith and trust in Christ began to grow and flourish again and at fifty-one he returned to the Shepherd and Guardian of his soul. He acknowledged his sin to the Carlisle congregation.

Afterwards his father wrote him a very different letter:

27 September 1990

My dear Son,

The Lord has answered my prayers for you. We both have had some painful years, a different kind of pain, but pain nevertheless.

There are several Scriptures that keep coming to my mind in respect to your returning to the fold – let me mention them for your encouragement.

Psalm 103:10–12: 'He has not dealt with us according to our sins, nor punished us according to our iniquities. For as the heavens are high above the earth, so great is His mercy towards those who fear him; as far as the east is from the west, so far has he removed our transgressions from us.' Particularly, verse 12. Don't let Satan depress you by past sins – you may still reap some of the scars but the sins are all covered in the 'all' of Psalm 103:3; also the 'all' in 1 John 1:7.

Another Scripture is Luke 7:36–48. Please note verses 47, 48: 'Therefore I say to you, her sins, which are many, are forgiven for she loved much, but to whom little is forgiven . . .' If David's sin had not been so great we would not have Psalm 51, the Psalm that is filled with sighs and tears. Dust had gathered on the strings of his harp which he played while he was sinning. There is no Psalmody in sin. Oh, how glad I am for this Psalm that consists in one long cry for pardon and restoration. Many a sin-tormented soul has found a path from a backslidden life to Christ through this Psalm. God brings good out of evil – a principle that is shrouded in mystery, nonetheless it is true. Without David's sin I do not believe we would have Psalms 6, 32, 38, 102, 130, or 143, and possibly 25, 69 and 86. David's sin also gave him unusual compassion for sinners and I trust it will be true of you – not sentimentalism but biblical compassion.

There is one other Scripture that has come to my mind, that concerns your future. You are 50+, and that may discourage you in respect to serving Christ. The Scripture is Matthew 20. The laborers in our Lord's vineyard, the ones who labored and began to serve him at the eleventh hour, were not paid less than those who went at the third, sixth, or the ninth hour. It is not length of service but the sincerity, the faithfulness, the consistency of the service that counts with the Lord. Our Lord did not serve long.

I believe God spoke to many people through your testimony at the church and I believe it is only the beginning of your usefulness in Christ's kingdom.

Would it be possible for you to come down for Thanksgiving or Christmas? Your mother and I are rejoicing in all current events – keep in touch.

The grace of our Lord Jesus Christ be with you.

Your caring father.

A month later Don replied to his father, and in the letter he said two things: 'First, I want to assure you of my deep and sincere love for you which never failed, even when at times (not many times) I appeared angry with you. I thank you most of all for caring for my soul as you have even before you were saved, since my birth and continuing since your conversion, through my life – all those prayers, tears, concerns and great letters over the years. Second, I want to thank you for your diligence and faithfulness as a servant of the Lord and as a winner of souls. Your service of the Lord and hunger for souls will always be an inspiration and encouragement to me as it is and has been to so many people. I need not, nor could not, list the people whose lives you have touched who remain faithful to this day. Praise God for Elmer.'

Throughout the ten years that, at this time of writing, have gone by since that letter was written, Don Reisinger has walked with God. He is his parents' counsellor, attendant and support in their infirmity. He bears with his father's bouts of irritability and anger! He cares for his mother. On one occasion he needed to write this letter of admonition to Ernie:

Sunday, 16 June 1991

Dear Dad,

After hearing you break down on the phone yesterday, you have been much on my mind, and I've tried to think of a way to encourage you so that you would not dwell on what you are no longer physically able to do. To this end, I've taken pen in hand to remind you of a few things that you already know very well.

1. Your physical frustrations could be coming from the Devil. He was a liar from the beginning and he is called the Accuser of the Brethren (*Rev*. 12:10).

2. Don't begrudge God for calling in some of the gifts that he has so graciously loaned you. 'He is an ill debtor who payeth back that which he borrowed with a grudge', said Samuel Rutherford. You have done well with the gifts God loaned you. You have done very well, with your life counting for God, by his grace and with his help. You have fought a good fight, you have run a good race. I wish to God I could say that.

3. You're not dead yet. Just because you are not physically able to occupy the pulpit any longer, aren't you still corresponding and sending out books to preachers, not to mention family readings? Aren't your tapes out there? Then you are still preaching, aren't you? Just because you are not on the battlefield doesn't mean you are not in the war.

4. The main thing I would like to remind you of is the wisdom and sovereignty of Almighty God. The wise man said in Ecclesiastes 9:1, 'So I reflected on all this and concluded that the righteous and the wise and what they do are in God's hands.' Psalm 115:3, 'Our God is in heaven; he does whatever pleases him.' Psalm 135:5, 'The Lord does whatever pleases him.' So it apparently pleases God to have public preaching virtually over.

5. Be ever thankful to God for the mighty way he has used you – ole' carpenter Ernie – and is still using you – all by his grace.

I trust that you will take these reminders to the throne of Grace with thanksgiving to God that he 'counted you worthy' to be used in his kingdom.

Thus end these fascinating letters which open some windows on a bitter-sweet relationship of two strong Christian men, father and son, which endures today. Don is now in charge of the *Christian Gospel Foundation* which distributes evangelical, Reformed and Puritan books world-wide, especially to ministers of the gospel. Since the 1990s many thousands of books and pamphlets have been distributed. This involves an enormous amount of correspondence, literally hundreds of letters to answer, and Ernie assists Don in this work.

17

THE GRANDCHILDREN

BY THE START OF THE TWENTY-FIRST CENTURY Ernest Reisinger had become a great-great-grandfather, with a family scattered across America, far away from Cape Coral, Florida, where he finally made his home. The grandchildren (Don and his first wife Patsy had six children) look back to happy vacations in Florida, going fishing together in the Keys: 'That's my most favourite memory of him', says Suzanne; while Christine writes, 'I am grateful to my grandfather for his many years of prayer for me and now my children and husband too. I know that he and my grandmother prayed for each of us by name daily, and for this I will be eternally grateful. I also have fond memories of visiting them over the summers and going out deep-sea fishing, playing games, and putting puzzles together.'

Don Jr. says, 'One of my favorite memories of my grandfather is that of our trips to Florida when I was young. On these trips we would listen to tapes of someone reading *Pilgrim's Progress*. After listening for some time Grandpa would shut the machine off and quiz us on what we had just heard. He then would tell us what it all meant. This is something that I will be for ever thankful for. It planted real seeds in my heart. Another favourite memory is when I was much older and had moved to Florida. My brother Jon and I would meet, and

Grandpa, to read and discuss Spurgeon's *Treasury of David*. This probably illustrates my Grandfather's greatest gift. He had a real strategy for witnessing the gospel. I am very thankful that the Lord blessed him in this way, because it led directly to my own conversion.'

Jonathan, too, sees such strengths in Ernie: 'In his ministry to the saints God has been pleased to use this man in an extraordinary way. My grandfather taught me a lot about having a strategy for witnessing. How we yearn to be used of God in these ways – to the saving of souls – to the praise of his glory. Often my Grandpa and I would sit and retell the stories of how God saved many friends and acquaintances along the way.'

All the grandchildren speak enthusiastically of Mima Reisinger. Elizabeth acknowledges, 'My grandma is a wonderful lady, very patient and very, very funny at times.'

Christmas time became one of the occasions Ernie would send letters to his young grandchildren. They reflect his own affection and seriousness. The following is a brief selection of his early family correspondence:

To his grandson Jon, Christmas 1979

Dear Jon,

We are certainly thinking of you and praying for you as we send this little gift. We did appreciate, very much, your nice letter and look forward to hearing from you again.

As we think about Christmas we also think of what it is all about – Christ coming into the world to reveal God the Father and to reconcile poor lost creatures to the great Creator – Immanuel - God with us. This knowledge of God has some fundamental principles. In reading a sermon the other day five of these foundational principles of knowing God were again brought to my attention. As a little Christmas message Grandma and I want to share these five things with you:

1. God has spoken to man, and the Bible is his Word, given to us to make us wise unto salvation.

2. God is Lord and King over his whole world. He rules all things for his own glory, displaying his perfections in all he does, in order that men and angels may worship and adore him.

3. God is Saviour, active in sovereign love through the Lord Jesus Christ to rescue believers from the guilt and power of sin, to adopt them as his sons, and to bless them accordingly.

4. God is Triune. There are within the Godhead three persons, the Father, the Son and the Holy Ghost, and the work of salvation is one in which all three act together, the Father purposing redemption, the Son securing it, and the Spirit applying it.

5. Godliness means responding to God's revelation in trust and obedience, faith and worship. prayer and praise, submission and service. Life must be seen and lived in the light of God's Word. This, and nothing else, is true religion.

We are happy to know that you are doing fine spiritually. And that you know it is a war with enemies on every side. We pray that our Heavenly Father will keep you, prepare you and use you.

We wish you could be here to pick some oranges from our trees. Maybe another year.

Keep up the good school work!! With much love.

To his grandson Jason, Christmas 1979

Dear Jason,

Thank you so much for your letter. We were very happy to hear from you and we are sorry we are a bit late in answering.

We are enclosing a gift certificate for Christmas, and as we do, our thoughts turn to the real meaning of Christmas, that is, why Jesus came – 'To save his people from their sins', and 'To seek and to save that which is lost.'

Our prayers for you this Christmas are that you would be seeking him as he is seeking you. We would encourage you and plead with you to seek the Lord while your heart is young and tender because if you delay, your heart will grow harder, and then, humanly speaking, it will be more difficult to be saved. God can and does save sinners at any age, but more often he seems to choose the time of youth. You will therefore understand our prayer for you at this season so that your young days will not pass over your head without you being saved, or that you will remember your misspent privileges if you are not saved at all.

We would love to be with you all at Christmas, but this must wait until another Christmas, if we are all here.

Wish you were here to pick some of our good oranges and grapefruit.

We both send our love and our kisses.

To his granddaughter Chris, Christmas 1979

Our dear Chris,

We are enclosing a little Christmas gift and, as we do we also send our warmest love. We wish we could be with you all at Christmas, however it seemed out of the question this year.

Naturally, when we think of you and Christmas we think of Christ, why he came and, his warm invitation to needy sinners to come to him and be saved.

We have many proofs that he is willing to save sinners. First, that he came at all. Second, his going to the cross. Third, his tears. Fourth, his words, *Luke* 19:41–42, 'And when he was coming near, he beheld the city, and wept over it, saying, If thou hadst known, even thou, at least in this thy day, the things which belong unto thy peace. But now they are hid from thine eyes.'

These words give us a little picture of his concern for all that belongs to our peace. We hear it in the carol, 'Peace on earth.' His coming and dying belongs to your peace – peace of conscience, peace in times of trouble and temptation – peace at the hour of death. And when you have Christ you have a peace that the world cannot give and cannot take away. On the other hand, without him there is no peace. The Bible says, 'The wicked are like the troubled sea when it cannot rest, whose waters cast up mire and dirt. There is no peace, saith God for the wicked.'

Christ said, 'O, if thou hadst known.' This shows a feeling of great love and tenderness, soon to be red with his own blood, and yet he wept over them.

Chris, we pray that with all the other joys of Christmas you might know not only 'Joy to the world', but joy and peace to your own souls.

We both love you very much – you have been the subject of many prayers.

Please write. We like to hear from you.

To his granddaughter Suzy, Christmas 1979

Our dearest Suzy,

As we enclose this little gift we are thinking of the real meaning of Christmas. That is, Christ coming into the world and why he came – to bring the peace and joy of salvation to the hearts and lives of all that come to him.

Suzy, our hearts are a little sad because we believe you once knew this real joy of Christmas and now you are not enjoying this peace and joy that only Christ can bring because you have turned from his way to your way like the disciples once did. But Jesus came to them again and he had to show them his hands and his side – and the Bible says, 'Then were the disciples glad when they saw the Lord,' (*John* 20:20). Their joy did not come from riches – their joy did not come from friends, or even family. Their joy did not come from looking at themselves, but when they saw his hands and his side which were wounded for them they knew the purpose for which he came was all completed. They saw the meaning of Isaiah 53:5, 'But he was wounded for our transgressions; he was bruised for our iniquity; the chastisement of our peace was upon him; and with his stripes we are healed.'

The disciples once had it and seem to have lost it. It was to them that Jesus came – 'Then were the disciples glad when they saw the Lord.'

O Suzy, we pray that as you hear about joy and peace of Christmas you will look again to Jesus and have true peace, true joy, joy that the world cannot give, joy that you will have not found since you turned away. May this Christmas bring the fulness of the real joy of Christmas you once knew to your heart again.

We wish we could be with you, but can only hope for another year.

We both send our warm greetings, love and prayers.

Love you much.

P.S. We have not received the long letter you said you mailed.

* * * * *

In 1991 Ernie began what he called 'Family Letters'. He had invested in his grandchildren's education at a Christian school, but many years had passed since their school-days, and the family were living in New York, Pennsylvania and Florida. Ernie felt he had been neglecting them. Some of the grandsons and their wives were at that time living in Cape Coral near him and their father Don. Ernie met two of them, Buzz and Jonathan, each morning for a hymn, a psalm and a prayer. So Ernie made a commitment that for fifty-two weeks he would send a letter to all ten of his grandchildren and great-grandchildren. Ernie used the fifty-two *Lord's Days* of the questions and answers in the *Heidelberg Catechism* as the foundation of all the letters. He supplied all the family with a copy of Ursinus's commentary on the *Catechism* – 'One of the five most valuable books that has ever crossed my path.'

The *Heidelberg Catechism* (1563) begins with the question, 'What is thy only comfort in life and death?', which it answers both magisterially and movingly, 'That I, with body and soul, both in life and death, am not my own, but belong to my faithful Saviour Jesus Christ; who, with his precious blood, hath fully delivered me from all the power of the devil, and so preserves me that without the will of my heavenly Father, not a hair can fall from my head; yea, that all things must be subservient to my salvation, and therefore, by His Holy Spirit, He also assures me of eternal life, and makes me sincerely willing and ready, henceforth, to live unto Him.'

The family received the following introductory letter from their grandfather: 'I am writing to ask you to join other members of the family in what I am calling, "A Family Reading". Each Sunday afternoon or evening we will all read the same *Lord's Day*. This will prove not only instructive to each individual but also good for the home and all our families. It should also provoke some wholesome discussions. Most of the fifty-two sections are less than fifteen pages, however there are a few that are longer. It will average about twelve pages per Sunday. If you have to miss a Sunday I suggest that you skip that *Lord's Day* so that you will be reading with the family. The starting date is Mother's Day, May 12. We will begin with Question 1 on page 17. I do hope that you will join us. In the meantime you may want to read the introduction.'

Ernie hoped it would provoke some wholesome and healthy Christian conversation in their homes between husband and wife and children, but if they only mastered the six pages of the first *Lord's Day* it would be worthwhile. 'You may find some things a little heavy or difficult, but let me suggest that you just bypass those things and make sure of this, that you clearly understand most of his expositions.'

The second *Lord's Day* the family received Ernie's letter which dealt with the next questions of the *Catechism*, that is, the misery of man, sin and its consequences. Ernie introduced the subject to them thus: 'When a physician is called to the bedside of a sick person, if he is an intelligent man, he will not only inquire after the nature of the sickness, but he will at the same time inquire after the cause of it. A doctor, who at once begins to write out a prescription, and immediately to administer medicines, without first investigating into the cause of your illness, I say such a physician is not worthy of your trust and confidence. If you are wounded, a good doctor will ask with what instrument you were wounded. If you have a disease, he will ascertain whether it is hereditary, and then will ask whether your parents or grandparents were ever stricken with the same disease. If you are ill, he must know something which may have caused your illness. When he has so examined you, and knows the nature, the cause, and the extent of your disease, then he will endeavor to decide upon the exact remedy. Now if all this is true with regard to our bodily diseases, then, it is yet more true with respect to the diseases of our souls.'

On the third *Lord's Day*, Ernie recognized that this was a long section, with Question 8 dealing with the bondage of the will. He sent them an additional pamphlet by Walter Chantry on man's will and pleaded with them, 'Don't let the length of *Lord's Day Three* discourage you from continuing with the Family Reading. We can come back to some things in this section later. I admit that there is some pretty heavy material in these expositions. It is not pabulum but all meat. Let me remind you of my motive, or aim, for these Family Readings. First, to introduce you to, and instruct you in the cardinal doctrines of the Word of God. Hence, it is not my aim to turn you into intellectual theologians who can argue all kinds of religious controversies – no, my aim is for each of you to achieve a sound doctrinal foundation on which you will build a solid and useful Christian life. The catechism summarizes, in a faithful manner, all of the fundamental teachings of the Holy Scriptures. Stay with us and you will be good informed Christians, and your soul shall prosper!'

Ernie returned to this theme on the fourth *Lord's Day*, saying, 'Catechetical truth is biblical truth, and this truth is not remote, abstract, or impersonal. No, no, this truth must become part and parcel of our lives; if not, all the instruction will be fruitless. We must make truth a part of our own lives, we must apply them in our daily lives. The biblical truths that we learn must mold our perspectives, shape our conduct, strengthen our commitment to Christ and his church and direct our endeavors in all areas.'

As with most things Ernie begins, he did complete all fifty-two letters, writing at their conclusion, 'I am aware that much of the exposition has been long and difficult, and I did not expect you all to master it now. It will be valuable all your life on important religious questions. As you travel on the road to eternity I hope you will first be sure of your own salvation and find comfort and joy in our God and Saviour.'

The attempt was over-ambitious, and, in structuring the children's Sunday afternoons, a noble failure. The children might have felt that they were being cajoled by Ernie into this programme, but his longing to see them growing in their grasp of truth was sincere, and this was recognized by them all.

Along with his strength, Ernie's grandchildren have also become aware of his weaknesses, as he himself acknowledges, 'I am sorry for many mistakes, for many words not spoken in love, for impatience with my family.' They have all witnessed Ernie in his eighties, angry, curt and dismissive, so that strains have entered their relationship with him. This has resulted in a certain coolness that their mother Patsy (Don's first wife) would long to see end. They all love their father Don dearly, and are sensitive to any instance of their Grandfather seeming to belittle his son. Jonathan Reisinger expresses it well when he says, 'One of the treasured quotes of my Grandpa's that I will pass on to my children and grandchildren is "the best of men are men at best". Often I hear people commenting in Sunday School as they read of the failures of one saint or another, "How could they do that?" We do no favors to any man when we elevate him above this earth. We all are but dust . . . The good news is that this is not the end of the story . . . not because of who we are, but because of what God is.'

Christine also longs that in these remaining years of her grandparents' pilgrimage all the family can get closer and focus on where God's grace has brought so many of them.

18

LIFE BEGINS IN FLORIDA

FLORIDA BECAME THE REISINGERS' PERMANENT RESIDENCE from the early 1970s. At first they lived on the Florida Keys, that line of low-lying islands that curve away to the south-west from the tip of the state for over a hundred miles to Key West and its international airport. Forty of those limestone islands are inhabited, and the road to Key West is 126 miles long and crosses forty-two bridges. It commences at Florida City, and the road is lined by green signs – the Mile Markers, starting with MM 126 at Florida City and ending with the final post at Key West which reads MM 0.

The whole area had an unspoilt character in those days. The Reisingers lived near Islamorada, a community about thirty miles from Florida City. The seas around Islamorada teem with gamefish – tuna, dolphin and sailfish on the Atlantic side, with tarpon and bonefish in the Gulf of Mexico. Coral reefs have made Islamorada a favourite centre for divers. There are nature trails in the state parks, and today shops and galleries line the streets of the town. Just off the coast is a little island with the highest elevation in the entire Keys – a dizzying eighteen feet.

A comparatively young man in his early fifties, Ernest Reisinger did not move south to rest on his oars. In their daily devotions he and Mima prayed that the Lord would both guide and use them. They were warmly welcomed to the First Baptist Church in Islamorada on their first visit. There were about a hundred people in the congregation, with a core of people who were serious about knowing the Bible. The church had services on Sunday morning and evening, with a Sunday School preceding the morning service.

They eventually became members of that church, and Ernie began to encourage the pastor of the congregation, assisting in some visitation, or in any way he could. They became friends and fishing buddies. Ernie provided some fine books for the young minister's library. The pastor soon took Ernie into his confidence, telling him that he was going to be leaving the church soon. When the young pastor went away candidating in other churches which were seeking a pastor, Ernie took the pulpit in Islamorada.

When the minister did leave Florida for a church in Georgia, the leaders in the Islamorada congregation invited Ernie to take on pastoral duties while they continued looking for a permanent replacement. They begged him to become their pastor, but Ernie never felt a call from God to that work and did not believe that he was their man. He did agree to fill the pulpit until they called a preacher. Once he had agreed to this they abandoned any serious search for a minister, so that Ernie occupied that pulpit there for three years. When he finally tendered his resignation a petition signed by every member of the congregation requested him to stay.

This was Ernie's first prolonged exposure to a church in the Southern Baptist Convention. This is the largest Baptist body in the U.S.A. with the names of fifteen million members on the rolls of about 38,000 churches. That also makes it the largest Protestant denomination in the States. Approximately half of all Baptists in America belong to churches affiliated to the Southern Baptist Convention. The work of the Convention is delegated to four boards, seven commissions, and six seminaries with over ten thousand students. It is somewhat of a missionary-minded denomination, supporting over three thousand workers in about a hundred countries.

During the time Ernie preached at the Islamorada church they distributed John Blanchard's *Right with God* to every home in the area. Ernie also broadcast a one-hour live radio programme each week. Some people were converted during this ministry, and one special encouragement came when Ernie befriended a young Pentecostal minister whom he met while fishing. As they would sit together on a boat they would talk for hours about the faith, Christian doctrine and church history. Ernie gave him many books by such men as Spurgeon, Ryle, Lloyd-Jones and Packer. The young man soon developed an appetite for all such books. It was not long before he had left the tongues movement and when he was baptized gave testimony to God's sovereign grace.

It was R. T. Kendall who had introduced Ernie to the delights of bonefishing in the shallow waters of the Florida Keys, and even Mima herself learned to fish for snook and redfish with her husband. Ernie was still musing over Kendall's thesis, 'The Rise and Demise of Calvinism in the Southern Baptist Convention'. The knowledge of the Convention's Calvinistic roots was to have an impact on the future course of his life, and on the denomination itself. Dr Kendall remembers those years, writing:

'In those early days when we first met, when Ernie and Mima came to see Louise and me in Florida, Ernie and I used to have prayer meetings together every morning. We would drive in his car to the beach in Fort Lauderdale as the sun was coming up and we would pray there together. I will never forget that as long as I live. I used to open my eyes and see tears rolling down Ernie's cheeks as he prayed. There aren't many people like that today . . . I salute Ernie Reisinger. I'm indebted to him beyond words . . . I thank God with all my heart for his influence on me.'

After Ernie completed his ministry at the Baptist Church in Islamorada he and Mima were uncertain as to where in Florida they would live. The character of the Keys was changing. Many refugees from Cuba had settled along the strip of islands and a prevailing Spanish-speaking culture was spreading throughout the islands' communities. The Reisingers took a trip and motored casually about Florida, wondering where the Lord would have them spend the next years of their pilgrimage.

One day they arrived at Cape Coral on the western coast of the state to visit some friends. At a restaurant they bowed their heads to give thanks for the meal and two strangers spotted them saying grace. They came across to the Reisingers and asked them, 'You are Christians?' 'Yes', said Ernie. In the ensuing conversation he told them that he and his wife were uncertain where to live and they were actually looking for a place to settle. 'This is the place for you', they said. 'You ought to look at Cape Coral. It's beautiful.'

The Reisingers never learned the names of these kind people, but that providential intervention meant Ernie and Mima did look around Cape Coral and they particularly appreciated its quietness. They were looking at the golf course and Country Club when nearby they saw a suitable house for sale which they proceeded to buy very quickly. So for a little time Cape Coral became their home, and from that community Ernie continued to send out literature all over the world and to fly off from the Fort Myers airport to preach across the U.S.A.

R. T. Kendall introduced Ernie to Al Dawson, Superintendent of Missions for the Gulfstream Baptist Association. After the Reisingers had been living in Cape Coral for a year, Dawson telephoned Ernie from Fort Lauderdale quite unexpectedly. 'I have fifty churches in this Association,' he said, 'eight of whom are without a pastor. Would you consider for my sake the needs of one particular congregation?' He mentioned a Baptist church in North Pompano, half an hour to the north of Fort Lauderdale. It had planted a mission church consisting of about one hundred people who were meeting at a school in a place called Margate. They had land, they had money and they wanted to build. Al Dawson thought that, given Ernie's years of experience in the construction business, he could guide these people through a building programme and preach to them at the same time.

Ernie found the idea intriguing, For the third time a group of people whose support he had in no way sought, had approached him: Mechanicsburg, Islamorada and now North Pompano. But eventually that mission church did not call Ernie to become their pastor. The pulpit committee consisted of six people, three from the mother church and three from the mission. The latter did not think Ernie was the man for this task, but the three from the mother church at North Pompano enthusiastically invited him to become their minister. The congregation had been without a pastor for a year, and they had been approached by thirty-five applicants before they called Ernie.

In June 1977 Ernie first preached there. He was fifty-seven years of age and had no idea of what he was getting into. Unbeknown to him the church had the most alarming problems. There had been four previous pastors, none of whom had stayed more than a couple of years, the difficulties thrown up by this group of people had overwhelmed those men, but Ernie remained there for eight years.

The church was teetering on the brink of disaster. Its paid staff was far too large for a church of that size. There were nine hundred names on the membership roll, but only one hundred and ten people were carrying the financial load of the church. The paid staff included a church secretary, a full time financial secretary, a paid pianist, a paid and untrained song leader, a full-time but utterly lazy caretaker, six or eight paid day-care teachers, a paid custodian for the day-care and a paid cook for the day-care. One of the first things Ernie did on arrival was to fire the caretaker.

Two weeks after he had settled into the church office the Power Company called to inform him that they were coming to turn off the power because the bills had not been paid. Here was a Christian congregation not paying for the electricity it was using while sending more than a $1,000 a month to the Southern Baptist Convention Cooperative Program. Next, the bank that was administering the church's $75,000 bond issue notified Ernie that they would no longer service the debt because the church kept making late payments, and the bank was fed up with receiving complaints from unpaid and disgruntled bondholders. This was the most serious financial problem facing the church. It would not have been easy to find another bank to service the bond issue, since only banks large enough to have trust departments were qualified to handle them.

But there was worse news to come. Ernie discovered that the financial secretary had been embezzling money from the church. The theft cost the congregation at least $23,000 and probably even more, but the church found it impossible to document the exact amount. The church held what it called a 'Make-up Sunday' whenever a looming financial crisis became too acute. This basically meant scraping an additional offering out of the faithful to pay some of its outstanding bills. This was the financial situation that Ernie had inherited unawares. 'God did not call me to be a fund raiser but to preach the gospel,' he muttered to Mima. But there was no way he could honourably jump ship and leave these people in this ungodly chaos.

The spiritual health of the congregation was far from good, and hardly prepared them for responsible stewardship. One by one he went through the names on the membership roll with two of the more knowledgeable men in the congregation. Ernie put an 'R' beside the names of all who attended church regularly – at least once a week. He put an 'O' beside the names of those who attended occasionally – once a month. He put a 'D' for 'delinquent' beside the names of all those they were sure had not attended, nor had any communication with the church, for a year or more.

That exercise was most revealing, and very sad. North Pompano Baptist Church had over five hundred and fifty religious delinquents, people who never darkened the doors of the church. Most of those people could not be traced. Of the nine hundred members on the roll less than two hundred and fifty bothered to show up on a given Sunday morning. A handful of people attended the Sunday night service, and about twelve to fifteen people turned up at the mid-week prayer meeting.

The church officers were all spiritually immature men. Six of the twelve deacons gave no evidences of conversion. The remaining deacons were doctrinally illiterate, that is, they simply did not know what it meant to be and act like a Christian. Most of the membership were in the same sad condition. There were even Sunday School teachers living in adultery, and this fact was known to the church members. After Ernie had been there for a short time one deacon's wife commented acidly, 'This preacher thinks the only thing we do right around here is to sin.' She was not far wrong. Ernie discovered, much to his dismay, that he was the pastor of a very run-down and dying congregation.

One mark of an evangelical church is that it is always reforming its life, and becoming more conformed to the image of the Son of God. The priorities of true reformation are personal holiness, obedience and understanding, not changes to the order of service and the structures of worship. There are not ten rules to guaranteed success in reforming a church, but there are some principles which Ernie has found helpful and that would save others from shipwreck. Ernie says, 'Most of these suggestions come from my own experience, and she is a queer old teacher. She first gives you the test and then the lesson.'

· Don't try to reform a church until you have first earned spiritual credibility.

· Study the biblical principle of accommodation. There are different degrees of growth in grace, and no saint is perfect in this life. Some Christians are able to receive more and to bear more because some are further along in growth than others. Furthermore, some Christians have more mental ability than others, some have more formal education, and some have had the high privilege of regularly sitting under a thoroughly biblical and consistently expository ministry. To deny the legitimacy or place of accommodation is to deny the obvious.

So the apostle, aware of the Corinthians' arrested growth in a specific area, could say, 'I have fed you will milk and not with meat; for hitherto ye were not able to bear it' (*1 Cor.* 3:2). Because the Corinthians were but babes in Christ, Paul adjusted their spiritual diet accordingly. He did not want to feed them that which they could not chew. So too, could Christ say to his disciples, 'I have yet many things to say unto you, but ye cannot bear them now' (*John* 16:12). To quote Calvin on this verse: as the disciples 'had nothing but his teaching to rely on, Christ tells them that he had accommodated it to their capacity'.[1]

· Three questions should be asked, and carefully answered, before implementing change: 1. What is the right, biblical thing to do? 2. How should change be implemented? 3. When should change be implemented? Don't try to do too much too soon. Many mistakes have been made by doing the right thing in the wrong way or at the wrong time.

· The principle of priorities must be applied. You can't change everything at once – first things first. Don't get hung up on secondary matters.

· The principle of the two churches must be before you at all times. There is the Ideal church conceived from the Scriptures and there is the Real church which you are pastoring. While the two will never meet on earth there is the joy of narrowing the difference between the two. You will work and pray,

[1] Reisinger commends an excellent message on this theme on tape by his present pastor, Thomas K. Ascol. This is available through the Christian Gospel Foundation, 521 Wildwood Parkway, Cape Coral, FL33904, USA, or Thomas K. Ascol, Grace Baptist Church, 204 SW 11th Place, Cape Coral, FL 33991, USA.

steadily, if at times it seems so slowly, to bring them closer together by raising the earthly imperfect one to the image of the heavenly one.

· Keep in mind the principle of church membership. Don't make church membership any narrower than the New Testament does.

· Remember the principle of restraint. Don't tackle the whole church at one time. Choose a few men who are sincere, teachable and spiritually-minded and spend time with them in study and prayer. They will help you to reform. This principle is found in Titus 1:5, 'The reason I left you in Crete was that you might straighten out what was left unfinished and appoint elders in every town, as I directed you.'

· In the pulpit, don't use theological language that is not found in the Bible. Avoid terms such as 'Calvinism,' 'Reformed,' 'doctrines of grace,' 'limited atonement,' etc. Most people will not know what you are talking about.

· Use sound literature, not indiscriminately, but wisely. Little things at first, that is, pamphlets and books with some doctrinal and experiential substance.

· Don't use the pulpit to scold people. You cannot scold people into reformation.

· Exercise common sense.

· Depend on the only weapons we have: prayer, preaching and teaching. As Oswald Allen puts it at the close of his hymn, *Today Thy mercy calls us*:

> When all things seem against us,
>   To drive us to despair,
> We know one gate is open,
>   One ear will hear our prayer.

· Be sure you understand the foundational doctrines and how they are related to each other and your situation.

· Check the history of your church to see whether it has any early constitutions or declarations of faith. Often you will find, particularly in older churches, a statement expressing the doctrines which you teach. A gracious appeal to such a document will give you credibility. At least your congregation will know you are not coming from Mars. Hide behind these articles of faith. Hide behind our Baptist fathers such as Bunyan, Spurgeon, Fuller, Boyce, Dagg, B. H. Carroll.

· Above all, remember that the proper motives for reformation are love to God and concern for his glory; love for man and concern for his good; love for God's holy law as the only perfect, objective standard of righteousness; love for Christ and his church; and love and compassion for sinners.

'Since nothing in this mortal life is more important than true religion in the soul and in the church, reformation should be diligently sought after, and carefully looked into. It is not enough to pout and complain about what is wrong with the visible church, but we must be preoccupied in reforming and restoring what is right and biblical. A censorious spirit will not reform the church.'

How did Ernie face this new challenge?

19

REFORMATION IN NORTH POMPANO

ERNEST REISINGER HAD LEARNED a simple formula in business for defining three activities necessary for success in any project: Analyse. Plan. Execute. He began in North Pompano Baptist Church by examining the church's staff, leaders and membership. He then adopted a plan of action, but where to start? The book of *Ten Easy Steps to Solve Church Problems* exists only in immature imaginations. Even if there had been ten such steps every preacher has to recognize the limitations set by man's inability. Ernie says: 'I knew those things I could not do: I could not change hearts, but God could. I could not give spiritual life, but God could. I could not open men's understanding, but God could. I could not give an effectual call, but God could. I could not reveal the truths of the Bible to the spiritually blind, but God could. I could not open the heart, but God could.'

Yet Ernie would not make his inability an excuse for inertia. He emphasizes as fiercely as any man that God uses human means to accomplish His purposes. The Pastoral epistles – Paul's letters to Timothy and Titus – are divine instructions to young preachers and they were a considerable help to Ernie during his years in North Pompano Baptist:

'I turned again and again to those inspired letters. As never before such verses as these just leapt from the pages of holy writ to my mind: "And a servant of the Lord must not quarrel but be gentle to all, able to teach, patient, in humility correcting those who are in opposition, if God perhaps will grant them repentance, so that they may know the truth, and that they may come to their senses and escape the snare of the devil, having been taken captive by him to do his will" (*2 Tim.* 2:24–26). These verses implied that three requirements were evident for an effective ministry in the North Pompano situation:

1. Acknowledging from the heart the true state of the unconverted, that they were in the snare of the devil, having been taken captive by him to do his will. Any superficial diagnosis would never reach the heart of the problem and would fail to provide the radical biblical cure.

2. Accepting the frame of mind which the New Testament teacher needed, that he cannot be quarrelsome or a man of strife. He must personally be gripped by the truth that he is teaching others. Above all, he must be patient.

3. Looking to God for results: the phrase 'if God' in *2 Tim.* 2:25 points to God's sovereignty. Ernie says: 'God may indeed grant repentance to sinners who are content to be the devil's captives. Hence, the Christian servant's confidence is not in his theological understanding, nor in the thoroughness of his preparation, nor in the subtlety of his wit, nor in the power of his persuasion. The servant's hope is in his God; that is an absolutely necessary persuasion and he must faithfully declare to the unconverted that their only hope of getting out of Satan's prison house is in the God who has the key to that

door, and the power to turn it. I placed those words of Paul to Timothy on my desk where I could see them every day.'

The most basic need of the people of North Pompano was a solid doctrinal foundation. They were, as a body, ignorant of the nature of Christianity, and the superficial superstructure that had been erected was falling apart. That crumbling religious structure was not surprising because any effort to be a practising Christian without a knowledge of what Christianity is all about will always fail. Ernie says:

'We live in a day of quick and inexpensive foundations, and our churches are collapsing as a result. Many congregations are full of carnal men, and carnal men do not want to be in the foundation business. They are not concerned with leaving a spiritual legacy for future generations. The only men who are interested in a true foundation are those who have their eyes fixed on eternity. Foundation work is laborious and costly. It is certainly not showy. Who wants to watch concrete poured into a footing? Foundation work is hard, dirty work. I was in construction for over twenty-five years. I know.'

Patience was also essential. Many a good plan has been aborted by impatience. The examples of men of God throughout history were ever before him. William Carey arrived in India on 7 November 1793 and Krishna Pal, the first convert, was baptized on 28 December 1800. Adoniram Judson toiled in Burma seven years before he harvested one soul. Robert Morrison sowed seven years in China before he saw one man converted. Robert Moffat waited seven years to see the first evident moving of the Spirit in Africa. Henry Richards spent seven long years in the Congo before he saw someone becoming a professing Christian.

What were these faithful men doing while they were waiting for results? They were patiently working, laying foundations, sowing seed, and focusing on future generations.

During his eight years at North Pompano, Ernie kept two churches in his mind at all times, according to his rule, already noted. One was the Ideal Church which is conceived in Scripture. If he had ignored that church he would have settled for the *status quo*. The other was the Real Church, the one he faced every Sunday morning at 11.00 a.m. The joy was in seeing the Real Church move toward the Ideal Church, at first in baby steps but soon in giant strides.

What means did Ernie use to bring about biblical reformation in North Pompano? He began with the leaders, meeting with the deacons, the leaders of the church and their wives every week for one hour before the Sunday evening service. In one year in this 'School of Deacons' he took them through the old London Baptist Confession of 1689. It was a significant beginning, and though some dropped out and left the church, about half of them completed this study of their unknown Confession of Faith.

What passages from the Bible should he expound to the church in his first year? Ernie chose the Sermon on the Mount in the gospel of Matthew chapters 5, 6 and 7. He had been blessed reading Dr Martyn Lloyd-Jones' *Studies in the Sermon on the Mount* (IVP). This book consists of a series of sixty sermons preached in the early 1950s at Westminster Chapel, London, when the minister was at the height of his powers. It has been an enormously influential volume. It portrays the beauty of a God-pleasing life and, incidentally, has done more to display the fascination and relevance of consecutive expository preaching than any other twentieth-century book. Ernie preached twenty-seven messages on the Beatitudes (with which the Sermon on the Mount begins), emphasizing Christ's teaching on the nature of a true Christian. By introducing the congregation to books like those of Dr Lloyd-Jones, Ernie took another step in church reformation. He set up his book table and commended special books each month to the people. Many thousands of books and pamphlets were distributed from that church table.

What was the response of the congregation to the 'School of Deacons', the vigorous systematic expository preaching from the pulpit, and the presence of a table covered with these challenging and yet inspiring books? It was as varied as the response in the parable of the sower. Some wanted to get rid of him. Others, by the grace of God, repented and began to hunger and thirst after righteousness. Then there were some who left the church. One man named David Clifton had been one of the most respected men in the church, having held every office in the congregation: chairman of the deacons, chairman of the pulpit committee and chairman of the finance committee. He had grown close to Ernie when, utterly unexpectedly, on 15 February 1979, Ernie received the following letter from him:

Pastor Ernie Reisinger
Fellow Deacons and Church Members
North Pompano Baptist Church

Dear Friends,

It is with very much searching of heart, Bible study, prayer and scientific research coupled with an air of sadness that I am persuaded to write this letter. My purpose is to be as honest and as open with you as I know how in expressing to you my present spiritual condition. This condition has caused me to conclude that I should resign as Deacon, Visitation

Leader, Chairman of the Nominating Committee and as a church member.

My present spiritual condition has resulted from a gradual deterioration of faith in the authenticity of the Bible over the period of the last year. I have discussed my condition with Brother Ernie several times over the last six months and he has tried to help me. I appreciate very much his efforts, but a change in my condition has not been forthcoming. I have not discussed this with anyone except my wife and I would rather not do so since in the process I might be tempted to defend my position and in so doing might cause someone's faith to be affected. My greatest concern in this announcement is that it might adversely affect some of you. I hope this does not occur.

I want to make it clear that I do not believe that the doctrines being taught by Brother Ernie and Brother Fred are unbiblical; on the contrary, I believe they are teaching exactly what the Bible teaches. My problem is not with the teachers but with the Bible.

I shall miss seeing each of you and I shall always consider you my friends.

Sincerely,

David S. Clinton

This letter was very painful to Ernie to receive. During the first year at North Pompano, Ernie felt he had aged ten years. Mima used to pity him as he left home each morning for the seven-mile drive to the church study. His routine was to arrive at 6 a.m. and use the early mornings for prayer, study and sermon preparation. He did not take calls until after 11.00 a.m., emergencies excepted. He then had devotions with other church workers, a psalm, a reading and prayer.

His weekly duties were as follows:

1. Prepare and preach three messages each week.

2. Prepare and teach the School of Deacons.

3. Attend hospital visitations (there were many elderly and retired people).

4. Conduct funerals (these were more numerous, given the elderly population, but they provided evangelistic opportunities).

5. Perform weddings (which he did not enjoy).

6. Edit a weekly four-page church paper, *The Good News,* which included writing a Bible Study for each issue.

The distribution of *The Good News* was especially profitable labour. At first they gave out 250 copies a week, but as other preachers appreciated the paper and wanted to use it, the distribution base grew to 1600. Ernie dealt popularly with big themes like the providence of God, divine sovereignty and human responsibility, and saving faith. Books were commended and the offer of a loan made to those who could not afford to purchase a certain volume.

There was also correspondence to attend to. Men wrote to him about problems in their churches. They were attempting to bring back their congregations to more biblical beliefs and practices and had not been as successful as Ernie. He would consider their trials and write his own biblical and common-sense counsel to them. Those who sought his advice before the issues became too intractable were saved much embarrassment. Those who wrote after their problem was too entrenched were given wise counsel on what to do next.

All his labours increasingly taxed Ernie to the limits of his endurance, and he was particularly thankful when the church called Fred Malone to become his associate minister. Fred is a gifted preacher and theologian who has written a little book on believers' baptism. Another man named Jim Carnes was also appointed in the spring of 1984 as a minister of Christian education. He took over the responsibilities of keeping the book tables stocked with new titles, corresponding with domestic and international publishers, as well as with individuals with specific needs. He saw this ministry grow in an amazing way.

Despite the hardships and disappointments there was much for which to praise God. Attendance at prayer meetings more than tripled. Attendance at the evening service doubled in size. The church debt was paid off and the mortgage payments completed. North Pompano sent out fine Christian literature to 3,200 Southern Baptist foreign missionaries in ninety-one countries, and to 2,400 home missionaries. The church also distributed a thousand copies of John L. Dagg's *Systematic Theology* and raised the money for its translation into Portuguese. It became the first volume of dogmatic theology available in the Portuguese language. Richard Denham, a respected missionary who has given his life to the service of the gospel in Brazil, visited the congregation. He placed before the church Brazil's need for such a book. This was announced one Sunday and the following Sunday an offering was taken. Almost the entire $15,000 was given for the cost of translating and printing Dagg. The generosity of this little congregation was exceptional.

Thus the church had turned in the direction of historic Christianity, but there is a sad note on which to conclude this summary of developments. Ernie tendered his resignation at the church and Fred Malone became his successor. After a short time, however, Malone left the area to return to study and work on his doctorate. Ernie was invited to occupy the pulpit again and another assistant was appointed who had been a church member for two years. This man remains a fine preacher and is soundly orthodox, but he was restless about the denominational affiliation of North Pompano Baptist Church, and he disagreed with Ernie's approach to leadership and church discipline. He wanted to take the church in another direction, and so a split took place, and about thirty good members of the church left under the leadership of the assistant to begin another congregation not many miles away.

A major point of difference focused upon the responsibility and authority of the elders, particularly in their role of shepherding individuals under their care. A tenet of Ernie's teaching was that the individual was free to grow and develop under the guidance of the Holy Spirit. In the light of a clear conscience he should apply the will of God to his life in an attempt – however feeble it might be – to please the Lord Jesus Christ, thereby growing in the knowledge and love for God. Ernie believed that elders should employ sensitivity and caution with respect to the privacy of the individual, using the preaching and teaching of the Word to transform lives. He believed in church discipline and exercised it at North Pompano, but reserved it for public sins that brought reproach on the name of Jesus. However, pressure was being exerted to expand elder authority. This different stance concerning the church's leadership was another part of the reason for the unfortunate division in North Pompano Beach Baptist Church. It was to become a formidable setback to the future life of the congregation. However, many of the achievements of Ernie's pastorate transcended that unhappiness, especially the remarkable distribution of one particular book, to which we must now turn.

20

JAMES PETTIGRU BOYCE

One of the lessons God taught Ernest Reisinger was the importance of literature in the spread of the gospel and the education of the church. From the commencement of his ministry at North Pompano Baptist Church he encouraged the congregation to become acquainted with books and pass them on to others: 'Anyone can prayerfully give away a good book. Books can be included in Christmas and birthday presents. Small booklets and tracts can be easily left with a gratuity (a generous, not a miserly one!) at a restaurant. Tracts can be included with letters and even bills that are paid by mail. As Robert Murray M'Cheyne said, "The smallest tract may be the stone in David's sling. In the hands of Christ it may bring down a giant soul." What the Puritan Thomas Brooks said of authors is also true of distributors: "Books may preach where the author cannot, when the author may not, when the author dares not, yea, and which is more, when the author is not."'

A seed planted in Ernie's mind germinated, grew, and prompted prayer and discussion with his co-pastor Fred Malone, until it sent down deep roots. Discovering the biblical foundations of the Southern Baptist Convention, Ernie had gathered from various used book depots a collection of the writings of the Convention's founders, and nothing impressed him as much as the 493-page volume written by James Pettigru Boyce in 1887 with the formidable title, *Abstract of Systematic Theology*. Dr Boyce was the principal founder of the first Southern Baptist Seminary during 1859, that great international year of revival. Boyce had entered Princeton Seminary as a student ten years earlier, and had come under the influence of men like Charles Hodge, Archibald Alexander and James W. Alexander. His theology had been clarified and strengthened, both by the instruction of these men and by their personal godliness. The years he spent at Princeton Seminary had been the most fulfilling experience in his life. His teachers had also become his role models, and he longed for what he had seen in New Jersey to be replicated in the South.

Dr Boyce presided over the Southern Baptist Seminary. He gave his life to it. Without his counsels and self-sacrifice the institution could not have survived the trials it endured, especially during the Civil War years or its move in 1877 from Greenville, South Carolina, to its present location, Louisville, Kentucky. He rightly said, 'The Seminary is my child.' Born of a wealthy family, Boyce gave sacrificially from his own inheritance to maintain the institution he founded. He had the utmost respect for Charles Haddon Spurgeon and eventually visited London during 1888, the last year of his life, and only four years before Spurgeon himself died. The great English preacher invited Boyce to speak at his 'Pastors' College'. Boyce's daughter, who was accompanying him, said that her father literally trembled and became short of breath when he met Spurgeon. Such was his admiration for Spurgeon that

Boyce muttered to his daughter afterwards, 'Compared to him, I have done nothing.'

Boyce's *Abstract of Systematic Theology* is the essence of his classroom teaching. He never thought of it as a deeply original or profound masterpiece, but simply as a practical textbook in the truths of the Bible, written for students and pastors who had not received seminary training, demanding enough from those who had had some theological instruction, but written lucidly to encourage those who were self-taught. It is judiciously and winsomely set out, and Boyce treats fairly those writers with whom he does not agree.

His own teaching reflected the truths he had heard as a boy in Charleston, South Carolina, and which were the means of his conversion in 1846. These convictions were further strengthened at Princeton, and, during his own years as a pastor, he preached increasingly clearly and effectively to the congregation of First Baptist Church, Columbia, South Carolina. He had not found the Bible's teaching on election an easy truth to accept. He finally was convinced that God's choosing man was an action of divine mercy shown to countless multitudes as numerous as the sand on the seashore. In other words, election was a display of the divine goodness to worthless rebels. Boyce took the biblical doctrine of sin seriously, at its face value. For almost thirty years of teaching he walked those 'old paths' and taught with a meekness and an earnest assurance that sovereign grace was God's means of ascribing glory to his Son Jesus Christ in the salvation of the world.

One particular student had to leave the Southern Baptist Seminary before the end of his course, and was able to return after a few years' absence. His anticipation, he said, was, 'to attend the "Systematic Theology" course and hear Dr Boyce pray'. Some of the men entering the Southern Baptist Seminary were Arminian, but during their years of study, when they heard Boyce expound the Bible, and witnessed his deep love for God – his great blue eyes gleaming as he looked at them – few were unpersuaded that this was the testimony of the Scriptures.

Several incidents indicate how Boyce's character as a man and a humble believer adorned the theology he made his own. His colleague, Dr John Broadus, was ill, and Boyce himself paid the expenses for him to enjoy a vacation. Arriving at the hotel, Broadus was too weak to climb the stairs to his room. James P. Boyce then lifted up his friend in his arms and carried him to his room. When Broadus later reflected on that incident and Boyce's character he said, 'He seemed strong like a giant, and he was as tender as a woman.'

As Ernest Reisinger read and admired James P. Boyce and his *Abstract of Systematic Theology* he was convinced of how valuable it would prove to the pastors in the Southern Baptist Convention. For many years the book had been ignored by all except the Landmark Movement. This was a nineteenth-century Baptist movement in the South which claimed that there had existed an unbroken succession of Baptist churches since the New Testament era. Its dominant figure was James R. Graves, who had been one of the most influential Baptist ministers in the nineteenth century in America. The Landmark Movement had printed *Abstract of Systematic Theology* with their own introduction, and Ernie bought the last 125 copies, but he could only use it with care because of its foreword.

'Why shouldn't we reprint it?' he thought. That could be done easily enough. But how best could it be distributed to those young pastors whose minds might be open to biblical influences? Why not reprint the book, and then each year give one free copy to every student graduating from the six official Southern Baptist seminaries and a few other schools? Surely this would bear fruit for the whole Convention. It would be an educational tool to instruct the denomination concerning the rock from which it was hewn; but this would also be living truth that sanctified and energized, so who could tell the spiritual good it might accomplish? It must be by truth, rather than programmes, that our evangelism and service to God are strengthened. Thus was born the 'Boyce Project' at the North Pompano Beach church.

As this particular congregation became more biblical in its attitudes it was, unawares, sharing with thousands of other Southern Baptist evangelical churches in a growing restlessness. There was a conviction in the U.S.A. that denominational leaders and seminaries had lost their moorings in the Bible and had drifted into modernist teaching. The spirit of evangelical Christianity in the 1970s could be summed up in the phrase, 'Back to the Bible'. These words had become the slogan of the biblical inerrancy movement. It was time in America for some costly reformation. The Missouri Synod Lutherans battled over the future of the Concordia Seminary in St Louis (1974). At the same time also the Presbyterian Church in America (PCA) came into being (December 1973). So it was an auspicious moment for the birth of the 'Boyce Project', so that it might benefit from the rise of this conservative movement for reformation and a return to historic Christianity.

The *Abstract of Systematic Theology* helped in some measure to shape a new ethos amongst the Southern Baptists where a number of the older conservatives in the denomination were not consistently Calvinistic.

Congregations of the Southern Baptist Convention all belong to a 'Cooperative Program' which requires massive financial support from the churches, proportional to the membership roll of the congregation. The money is sent from the local church to 'headquarters' and used to maintain the Convention's agencies and leadership. But it was there that theological liberalism was most evident; the agencies and seminaries were part of a problem no conscientious Bible-believing congregation could ignore. Rather than merely cut off the oxygen of financial support from the Convention's liberal agenda why shouldn't that Cooperative Program money – amounting to $13,000 in the case of the North Pompano Church – be spent on the 'Boyce Project' and thus be truly cooperative with the young men entering the Convention's pulpits and consistent with the truths loved by the very founders of the Convention? The North Pompano congregation agreed.

This gift of the Boyce book to all graduating seminarians also indicated Ernie's appreciation for his years of contact with the Southern Baptists, including his baptism in one of their churches shortly after his conversion, his initial membership in the first church he joined, First Baptist of Havre de Grace, Maryland, and happy memories of his years of ministry at First Baptist Church of Islamorada on the Florida Keys. The gift of the reprint and its free distribution was his way of saying 'Thank you' to the many evangelical Christians among the Southern Baptists. Ernie said, 'Many a life has been changed by one book.' He knew that this work of Boyce's did not contain 'new-fangled ideas belonging to some carpet-bagger who was a stranger to the Southern Baptist Convention', but it represented 'the best of our first founding fathers, the founding fathers of the first Southern Baptist Seminary, and we long to see those doctrines thundered through America. This is our desire; this is our motive; this is our longing prayer that God would be pleased to own this work to the glory of his great and holy name, and to the good of his church.'

When the book had circulated for some years, the fact that it did represent the pure origins of the Southern Baptist Convention was widely acknowledged. In 1982, Professor James Leo Garrett spoke to a class of students at Southwestern Seminary, Fort Worth, Texas, the largest seminary in the world with approximately five thousand students. Dr Garrett is the author of *Are Southern Baptists Evangelical?* and the massive *Systematic Theology: Biblical, Historical and Evangelical*. This latter work is exhaustive in its information especially concerning the teachings of twentieth-century theologians. Dr Garrett has been described as 'the ultimate research librarian'. Reviewers have grumbled that his *Systematic Theology* 'tends to read like a telephone book', and that 'the footnotes alone contain more information than the entire text of many works'. Garrett and Southwestern Seminary do not share the theological position of the North Pompano Baptist Church of that time, and that consideration might give his words more credence in the eyes of some. In a transcript of his taped lecture mentioned above we find the following remarks:

'Now, I want today to introduce some sub-types of Southern Baptist Theology. There are some movements that seem to be on the horizon. I call these sub-types because I am assuming (this may be a faulty assumption) that not one of these can really claim to be the majority belief of all thirteen million Southern Baptists. These are minority movements, or they are sub-categories; they are movements or they are teachings that have surfaced in Southern Baptist life enough that you can see them and detect them, but you do not know where they are going from here.'

The five movements within the Convention that Dr Garrett went on to discuss were: (1) the Charismatic Movement; (2) Dispensationalism; (3) the Biblical Inerrancy Movement; (4) the Keswick Movement; (5) the Calvinist Movement. About the last-named he said:

'Fifth: the Calvinistic Movement. Now, this is a movement that asserts the truth and the viability of the strong Calvinism that we can find in our Southern Baptist past and our English past. It is in a sense an effort to recapture the Calvinism that has been lost in the last three quarters of the century, or so, and to cover this involves a new emphasis on the writings of John L. Dagg and James P. Boyce and of the 1644 and 1689 Particular Baptist Confessions of Faith. The North Pompano Baptist Church in Pompano Beach, Florida, of which Ernest Reisinger is the pastor, now offers to give a copy of James P. Boyce's *Abstract of Systematic Theology* to every graduate of the six Southern Baptist Convention Seminaries and to Mid-America and Luther Rice Seminary graduates. So, when you graduate here, all you have to do is go by and sign your name and you'll get a free copy of Boyce, thanks to the North Pompano Baptist Church of Pompano Beach, Florida.

'Now, I would like to say that there is one difference that I can see between the neo-Calvinist movement and the other four. You may want to disagree with this, and that's all right. I believe that it differs from the other four in that it can more widely claim to be endemic to the Baptist past, the Baptist heritage and teachings of the past, than can the other four.

What I am saying is that whether we want to be Calvinists or not today, any serious study of our Baptist past must acknowledge that Baptists have been Calvinists. To distort that is to distort the records, it seems to me. So what I am saying is that it seems to me that the neo-Calvinist movement is able to say, "We are recovering part of our Baptist past", in a way that the charismatic movement cannot say it, because the charismatic movement represents something that is not endemic to the Baptist past. That has not been a common practice in Baptist churches through the years, and not been a teaching that prevailed . . . It is not a part of the Baptist past the way the Calvinist doctrine is. So I think I can draw that one distinction and be relatively fair in that assessment, and that dispensationalism as well is not endemic to the Baptist past in the same way that this new Reformed or Calvinistic movement is. I don't mean to suggest by that, that therefore it is valid and the other four not, in some kind of sweeping statement. I am simply making that observation.'

Ernest Reisinger appreciated that statement, only taking mild exception to the phrase 'neo-Calvinist movement', suggesting that a new type of Calvinism was emerging. Ernie believed that Dr Garrett would have been more accurate if he had spoken of 'paleo-Calvinism' (or old Calvinism)!

21

THE INFLUENCE OF THE BOYCE PROJECT

IT IS A TESTIMONY to the confidence in Ernest Reisinger displayed by the North Pompano Baptist congregation that so soon after his arrival as their pastor they could become enthusiastic about a project in which they were to give their money to distribute to seminary students a book with the forbidding title, *Abstract of Systematic Theology*. They believed that if this book could help produce a preacher like the one filling their pulpit then they wanted every Southern Baptist seminarian to read it. Commonly there is not a lot of interest or prayer in churches for seminaries. For pastors, evangelists and missionaries there is intercession, but those who teach in seminaries are not considered to be in the front line of Christian service and they tend to be ignored.

Publishing the Boyce volume required Ernie to initiate and sustain an enthusiasm in the congregation for a long-term project. It also demanded effort and sacrifice in its planning and execution. The money from the Cooperative Program, mentioned in the previous chapter, was not nearly enough to pay for the enterprise. More was needed. The church members bore the brunt of this. Ernie and the den Dulk Foundation undertook the details of the publishing, while finance came from sympathetic individuals such as Gladys Lee, Bill Menees and his wife, Harold Irwin and his wife, and the ever-supportive Grace Baptist Church of Carlisle, Pennsylvania. But many in the North Pompano church gave sacrificially to fund this project. There were even some elderly ladies who would purchase one book each month from their social-security cheques to give to a seminary student.

Six thousand copies of the book were initially printed and Ernie wrote to the six Southern Baptist seminary presidents asking permission to visit their campuses in order to present the volume to graduating students. Speaking in chapel at Southern, Southeastern and Southwestern was initially out of the question, but he received a cordial reception from all the presidents, even though in the late 1970s and early 1980s the men who held those offices did not take Ernie's side in the inerrancy debate. Later the official welcome in some seminaries distinctly waned. Initially Dr Russell Dilday, who was then the president of Southwestern Baptist Seminary, expressed his gratitude thus:

'Thank you again for what your church is doing in helping seminary students get acquainted with some of the classical books of theological expression. I have particularly enjoyed the David Ramsey's Founders Day address at Southern on Dr Boyce. Thank you for your interest and help. Our students certainly appreciate the generous gift,

Cordially,

Russell Dilday.'

The cordiality was later to vanish and the same president was to bar Ernie from distributing the Boyce book on Southwestern campus. It was reported that as a result of the distribution of the Boyce book discussions about Calvinism could be heard from the refectory to the Seminary's parking lot. However, both the seminaries at New Orleans and Golden Gate invited Ernie to speak at chapel.

Dr Paige Patterson, one of the most respected figures in the Southern Baptist Convention, consistently supported the distribution of Boyce. When president of Criswell College, he received the book warmly. He himself offered to present the book during graduation exercises, held as part of the regular Sunday evening worship service of First Baptist Church of Dallas, which was broadcast live across the city. This broadcast exposed the book to more than 30,000 people. Dr Patterson invited Ernie to speak at a chapel service and ensured that the book was regularly sold through the Criswell Center bookstore.

In the 1978–9 school year alone, the North Pompano Baptist Church distributed over 2,000 copies of Boyce's book. By the end of 1980, the church had distributed over 5,000 copies, and Ernie and Fred Malone had received hundreds of encouraging letters from the graduates who had accepted them. They continued the project in 1981, giving away over 1500 copies that year. All in all, the church ended up reprinting over 12,000 copies of the *Abstract of Systematic Theology*.

Over the course of three years Ernie travelled over 25,000 miles, giving out Boyce volumes to seminary graduates. The cost was over $100,000 for printing, travel, airfares, etc. Ernie flew to Southeastern Baptist Seminary in Wake Forest, North Carolina, New Orleans Baptist Seminary in Louisiana, Southwestern Baptist Seminary in Fort Worth, Texas, and Golden Gate Baptist Seminary in California. It was particularly moving for him on the first occasion he went on campus at the Southern Baptist Seminary in Louisville to see the Boyce Library. His photograph was taken in front of that beautiful building as he presented the incumbent president, Duke McCall, with a volume of Boyce.

It was one thing, however, for a graduating student to be willing to receive a gift, another for there to be the incentive to read it. Students commonly bought many books during their years of studies and yet did not read them. And a free book does not create the same inducement for reading as one which a man has bought. There might, of course, be a winsome chapel presentation of the book – which Ernie did so well – but many seminarians missed the opportunity of hearing him, or any chapel preacher, speaking. So what he and Fred Malone did was to distribute this note to each recipient:

'I am writing this letter to take a little survey of opinions on a few of the chapters in Boyce's *Abstract of Systematic Theology*. For your cooperation in this survey we will send you a free copy of the Old Baptist Confession of 1689, later adopted by the Philadelphia Association out of which the Southern Baptists came. These are the questions:

· Do you believe that Dr Boyce is biblically correct in his chapter on Effectual Calling (Chapter XXI – page 367)?

· Do you think his view of the Doctrine of Election is the biblical teaching (Chapter XIX – page 341)?

· In Chapter XXVIII – page 295, Dr Boyce sets forth several views of the Atonement. Which view do you believe to be the biblical view?

· Please comment on Chapter XII – page 106, The Will of God.'

That this shrewd questionnaire was an encouragement to some others to read the book cannot be denied, but the whole conviction of Boyce's book itself is that, when men have done all they can to commend God's truth to the world, it is the Lord alone who can open the understanding, and, furthermore, that God does so when he is pleased to do it. That is his grand prerogative, and in that honour none shall share. Professor Don Whitney of Midwestern Baptist Seminary, a former student at Southwestern Baptist Seminary in 1979, attests to this experience:

'Late in April 1979, I was walking through the Student Center at Southwestern Baptist Theological Seminary in Fort Worth, Texas. A man with a box of books at his feet asked if I were graduating next month. When I told him I was, he offered a copy of the book provided I simply read a few specific pages and responded in writing to a sheet of accompanying questions. I paused, knowing that I wouldn't have time to complete that assignment during the last week of school, but finally agreed on the condition that I should fulfil their request in a few weeks. Later that day, back in my apartment in Irving, I placed my new copy of James P. Boyce's systematic theology on a bookshelf. I can still see it pulled halfway out of the shelf, my self-reminder to keep my word about the reading and responding.

'Sometimes during the summer I found the time to take down the book and read the section selected for me. Out of sheer obligation I finished the pages and dutifully wrote my answers to the questions. The heart of my response was: "Thank you for the book. But Boyce's views in this passage cannot be true, for if he is right then there's no such thing as free will." ("And", I implied, "everyone knows that we all have a free will.")'

Ernie Reisinger well remembers the green ink Don Whitney used in writing this letter, and his beautiful script in answering the four questions, though every answer was wrong. But the story is not all told. Dr Whitney continues:

'In January of 1980 I assumed my first pastorate, a country church near Arkadelphia, Arkansas. Shortly thereafter I began preaching through the book of John in the morning and Ephesians in the evening. By the time I got to Ephesians 1:4, I had to deal with the subject of election. I decided to check everything I could find in my library on the subject. I remember locating twenty-nine different sources which deal with the issue, from commentaries to systematic theologies, including the book by Boyce. As I read, a change began to come over my thinking. Previously I had believed that the doctrine of election was either true or false. Now I realized that was a false dichotomy. EVERYONE I read believed that the Bible taught election, they simply differed on *what* it taught. It dawned upon me that, after all, 'election' is a Bible word, not a word developed by theologians.

'My second encounter with Boyce was to read with new eyes. This confrontation with the Scriptures on the subject, and the arguments of men such as Spurgeon and Boyce, shattered my preconceived ideas about and prejudices against the sweet doctrine of God's sovereignty in choosing whom he will to salvation.

'For the first time in my life I think I understood grace. I thought back to my conversion at age nine. When I was six I had a long illness which could have killed me, and was nearly run over by a car at age seven. I realized that had not the Lord spared my life, and then drawn me to himself, I would have been at that moment a young boy in hell, and deserving to be there. Previously I would have thought as many do (though no one would be crass enough to say it) that, "Yes, the Lord saved me, but at least I had enough sense to know what to do when I heard the gospel." Now I realized that I had contributed nothing to my salvation but my sin, and that God had no obligation to save me or even to allow me to hear the gospel. I had nothing to offer him, no claim upon him. He saved me purely out of his sweet sovereign grace and mercy,

'I put my head down on my desk that February morning in 1981, and sobbed convulsively over my sin, presumption, foolishness, and the wondrous, free grace of God.'

Since that time Don Whitney has pastored a church in Illinois for many years, and now he serves as a professor at Midwestern Baptist Seminary in Kansas City. He has become the author of some excellent books, *Spiritual Disciplines for the Christian Life*, *Spiritual Disciplines in the Church*, *How Can I Be Sure I'm a Christian*? and *Ten Questions to Diagnose Your Spiritual Health* (all published by NavPress).

Dr Tom Nettles was also met by the distribution of the Boyce volume, although he was a professor rather than a graduating student. Converted in August 1969, he read voraciously. Before a year was out he had devoured *Evangelism and the Sovereignty of God* by J. I. Packer, *Baptist Confessions of Faith* by W. L. Lumpkin, and W. T. Conner's *Gospel of Redemption*. These books had persuaded him of the truth of the doctrines of God's sovereign grace. When he became a theological student he heard about John L. Dagg and James P. Boyce. When his professors mentioned these men they merely said that they represented 'the old position'.

When he checked out their theologies he discovered that they taught the same truths as the old Baptist Confessions. Nettles was surprised to learn how widespread Southern Baptists' belief in the doctrines of grace had once been. Few other men, staff or students, seemed to be interested and Nettles thought his own future would mean ploughing a lonely furrow. For a time he did not encounter the activities of the Banner of Truth Trust, knowing only of Jay Green's republication of the old works. Southwestern Baptist Theological Seminary was drawn by Nettles' academic qualifications, attractive personality and preaching skills, and in January 1976 he was invited to join their faculty in Fort Worth, Texas.

At Fort Worth, Tom Nettles came to hear of a certain church in Florida that distributed Boyce's *Abstract of Systematic Theology* to all graduating students. He thought it was a noble ideal, but felt that it would bear little fruit and eventually fizzle out. How could there ever be in the Southern Baptist Convention a significant response to these truths? Surely students who adopted them would become totally marginalized in remote places and have to endure their ministries being represented as curiosities. Nettles had not yet become a reformer or guessed the wide attractiveness and relevance that the doctrines of grace might have for every single congregation.

Ernest Reisinger heard of this interesting lecturer from a student in 1977 and sent him a couple of boxes of Banner of Truth books including the *Works of Jonathan Edwards*. Tom Nettles says, 'I was overwhelmed. Quickly browsing through the treasure I discovered that a massive amount of godly pastoral, doctrinal and sermonic material was available written from this viewpoint and that Ernie was in part instrumental in their publication and distribution. Ernie also included his own booklet on *What Should We Think of the Carnal Christian?* I read it immediately, and discovered that Ernie set out what I had been thinking and had begun to teach. I wrote to him for advice on a couple of issues of interpretation.'

In the spring of 1977 Ernie visited Texas to distribute the Boyce books. He was staying in a campus room at the Southwestern Seminary, and to reach his room in the evenings he had to walk past the switchboard. He noticed that each time he went by the counter the student telephone operator's nose was in a book. After his initial smiles of greeting Ernie finally stopped and said to the young man, 'Are you studying for an exam?' 'Yes,' he replied, adding 'for the best professor on the campus.' 'Who is that?' asked Ernie. 'Dr. Nettles', he said confidently. Other students agreed with this assessment, not necessarily accepting what they perceived to be Nettles' theology, but appreciating his spirit and teaching gifts.

The next day Tom Nettles and Ernie met for the first time. Tom Nettles remembers the occasion: 'I will never forget how warm, friendly, prayerful, challenging and solicitous of my well being he was. It was clear that Ernie loved God, loved his truth, and loved his servants. More books followed, as well as an invitation to come to Pompano to preach. More books were given to me there, especially Thornwell's *Works*. My heart became wed to Ernie's and I was greatly strengthened to teach the truth of the gospel and encourage young ministers to endure hardship as good soldiers of Jesus Christ. On one of the visits Ernie made to Fort Worth we had a meeting in our home in which he spoke to several seminary students and encouraged them with the power of literature. He was always reminding us to employ "those twenty-six soldiers"[1] on the

[1] See also p. 239.

side of truth. He also spoke in several of my classes. All this began to increase the interest of Seminary students in the doctrines of grace.' It sounds as if there were more car-park discussions on Calvinism! Today Dr Tom Nettles is the Professor of Historical Theology at Southern Baptist Seminary in Louisville.

Encouraged by the benefits of the Boyce project, Bob Selph, at that time the pastor of the Miller Valley Baptist Church in Prescott, Arizona, determined to distribute to all Southern Baptist pastors a small book he had written entitled, *Southern Baptists and the Doctrine of Election*. Again it proved educational and informative to the denomination's pastors. The Yavapai Baptist Association were so ignorant of their roots that they charged Bob Selph with heresy for promoting the teaching of unconditional election. He was subject to formal proceedings that stopped short of removing him and his church from the association. In 1993, the same association adopted a resolution repenting of this sin against Selph and his congregation.

22

THE FOUNDERS' MOVEMENT

THE PERSONAL CONTACTS Ernest Reisinger made from his travels distributing the Boyce volumes throughout the seminaries of the Southern Baptist Convention could be numbered in the hundreds. The end of the 1970s and the entire decade of the 80s was a fertile period for the spread of free-grace teaching in the U.S.A. The divinely-set time for this resurgence had come, and Ernie could count on a number of contributing influences. The writings of J. I. Packer, R. C. Sproul, James Montgomery Boice and Martyn Lloyd-Jones, the preaching of Al Martin, the growing influence of John MacArthur, and the teaching of conservative Presbyterian seminaries were all encouraging the revival of experiential Calvinism. From the United Kingdom, Banner of Truth books were slowly spreading among American churches.

Fred Malone and Ernie received letters and telephone calls from hundreds of young Southern Baptist pastors seeking help in applying the truths of God's sovereignty to their ministries. Especially from their pulpits in evangelism, they wanted to know the implications of the doctrines of grace for fervent soul-winning. But also with respect to living the Christian life, house-to-house personal work and counselling, their question was, 'How does Puritanism apply to the American church today?' The following letter, written to Ernie by a pastor in Cascilla, Mississippi, is typical:

'I came to embrace in my early years as a Christian some of the truths of the 'doctrines of grace,' and have attempted, especially since entering the pastorate about a year ago, to implement these theological understandings into the work of evangelism. I find myself the pastor of a rural church in Mississippi which is basically untheological in its approach to Christianity and church order and practice. Of course, where there is dwarfed understanding of the doctrines of the Bible there is consequent shrinking of the spiritual life of the church members.

'I must also confess that I, as a pastor, am not completely clear in my own mind as to the proper approach on the practical level to evangelism and church order. I am well versed in the 'decisionizing process' . . . and am dissatisfied with its fruits, but am not ready to discard the invitation system completely. My problem is that I have never seen a church which embraces the work of evangelism and has instituted church order from this biblical standpoint while remaining fervent and experiential in its outworking of the Christian life . . . Could you help me? How do you lead folks to a conversion experience without 'decisionizing' them? Applying the emphasis you speak of on teaching, when and how do you lead the sinner to close with Christ? Realizing that baptism is the biblical way of confessing Christ as Savior and of identifying with him, how does a church accept a person as being a proper candidate for baptism? How do you do this in a congregation which would consider the discarding of the invitation system as heresy and has such a low view of conversion and regeneration and no concept of biblical church order? Could you make an attempt at answering some of these? I realize that some of them are matters of practicality, but I am a bit perplexed as to how to proceed.

'P. S. Do you know of any churches and pastors in this area which are concerned with reformation in the local church which I could have fellowship with?'

Such queries from younger preachers called to pastor traditional congregations were not infrequent. Almost all of them had inherited the so-called 'altar call' which in the Southern Baptist Convention has become as much a part of the worship service as the reading or the pastoral prayer. How could they reconcile it with their convictions about the free grace of God saving men?

Though he was no supporter of the invitation system of evangelism Ernie always urged preachers to introduce changes wisely, and not to override the consciences of people where they were still bound by ignorance or misunderstanding. He would urge them to consider the implications of the words of the apostle Paul: 'Be careful, however, that the exercise of your freedom does not become a stumbling block to the weak. For if anyone with a weak conscience sees you who have this knowledge eating in an idol's temple, won't he be emboldened to eat what has been sacrificed to idols? So this weak brother, for whom Christ died, is destroyed by your knowledge. When you sin against your brothers in this way and wound their weak conscience, you sin against Christ. Therefore, if what I eat causes my brother to fall into sin, I will never eat meat again, so that I will not cause him to fall' (*1 Cor.* 8: 9–13).

At the same time Ernie warned against any compromise which involved the relinquishment of Christian principles in order to accomplish certain purposes. There is certainly the invitation of the gospel to all men to come now to Christ. One result of embracing the Reformed faith must be an increase of evangelistic ardour or enterprise, or one has not understood the faith that so empowered Edwards, Whitefield, Carey and Spurgeon. There is place for a free welcome to any in the congregation to come at the end of the service and speak further to the preacher concerning what has been heard in the sermon. That combination of urgent exhortation, and willingness at that moment to assist any conscious of spiritual need, might be enough to satisfy many Southern Baptist congregations. The church would see and know that their preacher did believe in a gospel freely offered to all men. 'You may need to find ways to engage in some personal restraint without compromise particularly in those early years of your ministry', Ernie would write to young ministers.

Ernest Reisinger began to gather from his correspondence the names of Southern Baptist pastors who were sympathetic to the doctrines of grace. By July 1982 he had an informal network of over 500 preachers with whom he was making contact by mail or phone, at least twice a month, to discuss their mutual interest in the theology of such Southern Baptist fathers as Boyce, Broadus and Dagg. On 6 October 1982 he sent the following letter to pastors who shared an interest in reformation in the denomination:

'This is a form letter and I am sorry I do not have time to write a personal letter at this time. However, I would really appreciate your cooperation. There are increasing numbers of men amongst Southern Baptists who have come to a knowledge of those great truths of our founding fathers. John A. Broadus, in describing the theology of Dr. James P. Boyce, called these truths "that exalted system of Pauline truth which is technically called Calvinism". I have quite a few names and there must be many more.

'Several persons have expressed a desire that we compile a mailing list of such men within the Southern Baptist Convention. The immediate purpose would be so that we could have some contact with each other and possibly recommend such men to churches in our various associations that are without a pastor. Also we could recommend the men and their churches to our own people who are vacationing, or moving and seeking a church that holds to the biblical truths of our Baptist fathers.

'Secondly, we may be able to have a little newsletter every three or four months in order to keep in touch with each other. Definitely not to form an organization or party, but principally for acquaintance and fellowship.

'Your name has been given to me by a mutual friend so I am writing this letter to ask if you would send me the names and addresses of men in the Southern Baptist Convention that you know who believe the doctrines of grace, or are sympathetic toward these doctrines. For this assistance, I will send you the list of names when it is compiled. I am enclosing a copy of our church paper, *Good News*. If you would like to be on our mailing list for subsequent copies, please advise.

'With warm Christian regards,

'Sincerely yours in Christ's service according to my light and power,

Ernest C. Reisinger.'

Tom Nettles and Reisinger had for some years discussed the possibility of holding a conference. Nettles was receiving many phone-calls and much mail about the issues which the doctrines of grace raised in pastors' minds. After much hesitation, and even travail of soul, a meeting was held in November 1982 at a Holiday Inn near Dallas, Texas. Ernie, Fred Malone and Tom Nettles were present, along with three of Nettles' former students, Bill and Tom Ascol and Ben Mitchell. They spent the first half of the day praying and reading psalms and hymns. It was one of the most humbling times of prayer the men had experienced, with a consciousness of God working through them and being with them.

In the afternoon they discussed the direction in which God might be directing the spread of his truth in the Southern Baptist Convention and how they might become more effective as his fellow-workers. They finally settled on the idea of a conference with the doctrines of grace at its heart. It would be known as the Southern Baptist Founders Conference. Its purpose would be to promote historic Christianity, especially in the experiential application of its truths to local church worship and witness. A variety of speakers would be invited to present formal papers, sermons, expositions and devotions; literature would be promoted and sold, friendships and fellowship encouraged. Thus Southern Baptists would be inspired by the Word of God to honour his gospel more perfectly and make his church stronger.

The first conference was planned with some trepidation, which increased as 1–4 August 1983 got nearer. It was held on the campus of Southwestern University (now Rhodes College) in Memphis, Tennessee. The speakers and their subjects were as follows: '*Pilgrim's Progress* and Teaching Grace' (James D. Gables); 'Meditation from Psalm 80' (C. S. Storms); 'Life and

Labors of P. H. Mell' (Ben Mitchell); 'Sovereign Grace in Romans 8 and 9' (Richard P. Belcher); 'The Doctrines of Grace in Baptist History' (Tom Nettles); 'The Doctrines of Grace in Church Planting' (George McDearmon); 'Doctrine and Devotion' (Ernest Reisinger); 'The Lordship of Christ' (David Miller); and 'The Effective Call' (James Millikin).

Many testimonies were given, both in session and in personal conversation, about the impact of the Boyce project on the ministries of young preachers. The Founders Conferences never looked back from that first blessed week, and they have continued annually ever since. Until 1991 the conferences were held in Rhodes College, Memphis. Since 1991 they have been held at Samford University in Birmingham, Alabama. In 1998, 560 people attended, while in 1999 almost 600 were present, with John Piper as one of the speakers. In 1987 a youth conference was initiated, led by Bill Ascol, and that has continued to meet. In 1990 a quarterly magazine, *The Founders' Journal,* edited by Tom Ascol, was launched. Twelve hundred people receive it; and in 1995, the Southern Baptist Sesquicentennial year, an issue of the magazine was sent to every pastor, missionary and professor in the Southern Baptist Convention. There is also a web page, *Founders Online* at www.founders.org, while the Founders Press is the latest advance, with the first trickle of publications.

For ten years Ernie Reisinger chaired the Founders Conference planning committee. He says, 'There is no doubt in my mind that a real reformation in Southern Baptist life is in progress, and I believe the Boyce book and the Founders Conferences are no small part of what is going on.' Dr Tom Nettles has spoken of the Boyce project in these terms: 'A just consideration of the dimensions of influence carved out by that one theology book, barely sketched out in places, and readied for publication only shortly before Boyce's death, exhilarates the imagination. The wisdom from above given to Ernie in settling on that particular ministry has borne good fruit. *Soli Deo Gloria!* By God's grace that initial project has resulted in Boyce's theology again being taught at the Southern Baptist Theological Seminary, as well as Midwestern, and serving as a challenge for the other seminaries to expand their awareness of our theological heritage.'

The impact of the spread of Boyce's theology can be seen in the consequent outbursts of criticism of Calvinism in particular, some of which were focused directly on Ernest C. Reisinger. Dr William R. Estep, emeritus professor of church history, Southwestern Baptist Theological Seminary, levelled a broadside at him by name in an article published in the *Texas Baptist Standard*.[1]

He accused Southern Baptist Calvinists of having 'only a slight knowledge of Calvin or his system', and of 'simply borrowing that which they assume to be both biblical and baptistic without adequate research'. He contended that the Calvinistic system was 'without biblical support'. It arrogantly assumed 'to know more about the purpose of God and the eternal decrees upon which it is based than God has chosen to reveal in Scripture or in Christ'. Its advocates worshipped a God who 'resembles Allah, the god of Islam, more than the God of grace and redeeming love revealed in Jesus Christ'. Its view of human responsibility made 'a person into a puppet on a string or a robot programmed from birth'. It was 'anti-missionary'. Its proponents historically had been 'marked by intolerance and a haughty spirit'. In sum, according to Estep,

[1] William R. Estep, 'Doctrines Lead to Dunghill, Prof. Warns', *Texas Baptist Standard*, 26 March 1997.

'If the Calvinizing of Southern Baptists continues unabated, we are in danger of becoming "a perfect dunghill" in American society.'

These words did not need to be answered by Ernie himself. A number of men leapt to defend him and the truth. Dr Tom Ascol wrote in the *Founders' Journal*:

'The topic which Estep addresses is an important one and should be discussed. But such discussion ought to be conducted on a high level, working diligently not to misrepresent those with whom we disagree, seeking not only to be understood but to understand, and with renewed commitment to love the brethren – even those, perhaps I should say especially those, who differ with us theologically.'[1]

Dr Albert Mohler, the President of Southern Baptist Theological Seminary, also responded to Dr Estep's words, saying that if this were a true representation of Calvinism he would want nothing to do with it: 'Nevertheless, few of Calvin's friends or enemies will recognise Calvinism as presented in Estep's article.' Dr Roger Nicole also answered Estep in the form of a 'Dear Colleague' letter, dissecting the original article sentence by sentence, and concluding, 'I do find comfort in the thought that although you may oppose Calvinism on this earth, you will yourself be a Calvinist when you get to heaven, for I say, who will deny or seek to restrict the sovereignty of God when appearing before his throne?'

Dr Adrian Rogers is the pastor of Bellevue Baptist Church in Memphis, Tennessee. His church has grown from 9,000 members in 1972 to more than 26,000 members today. A staunch defender of biblical inerrancy, he has thrice been

[1] Tom Ascol, 'Do Doctrines Really Lead to Dunghill?' *Founders' Journal*, Summer 1997.

appointed the President of the Southern Baptist Convention. In his correspondence, sermons and pamphlets he seems to delight in placing Baptist Calvinists in the worst possible light by using unrestrained language to describe fellow believers whose chief desire is to understand and obey the Word of God. For example, irresistible grace, he says, means that God is 'going to zap you . . . no matter what'. Calvinists are the 'chosen frozen, the elite, the satisfied, the cheese and wine theologians'. On 13 March 2000, he preached a radio message in which he dubbed belief in unconditional election as 'libel against God'. He accused Ernie in correspondence of having 'more zeal for the cause of Calvinism than for missions and evangelism'. He equated the God of Calvinism with the god of Islam and stated, 'I refuse to let my church be dampened down by a form of incipient fatalism.'[1]

Another evangelist from Texas, Freddie Gage, declared: 'There is not a nickel's worth of difference between liberalism, five-point Calvinism and dead orthodoxy', because all are 'enemies of soul-winning.'[2]

Such high feelings indicate that the free-grace movement amongst the Southern Baptists is no longer the conviction of a few curiosities living on the frontiers, but it has come into the mainstream of Southern Baptist life. The Lord once described as blessed men those people who are being insulted and to whom are falsely attributed all kinds of evil. We are to 'rejoice and be glad' whenever this happens, Jesus said (*Matt.* 5:11–12). Charles Haddon Spurgeon had that text on his bedroom wall. Ernest Reisinger has cause for joy.

[1] Copy of letter to Ernest Reisinger, 18 February 2000.

[2] Mark Wingfield, 'Gage: Baptist churches are not reaching "pagan" culture', *Baptist Standard*, 24 April, 2000)

23

ERNEST C. REISINGER: AUTHOR

FORMIDABLE PUBLICATIONS from the pens of preachers such as Francis Schaeffer and D. Martyn Lloyd-Jones did not begin to appear until the authors were mature men, and then a flow of books commenced which was worth waiting for. They represented the considered thought of evangelists who, after years of active Christian work, had either taken up the pen, or permitted others to transcribe their messages and form them into books. Ernest Reisinger came late in life to writing anything. After almost forty years of Christian living, his first book, entitled *Today's Evangelism: Its Message and Methods* (Craig Press, Phillipsburg, NJ 08865) made its appearance in 1982. Ernie's chief gift lies in his power of exhortation; that is, he is able to take a familiar biblical theme, often some great concept of God, and use it to stir the affections of a congregation to fall in love with that truth, or rediscover it in a fresh way. He is a warm and personable speaker, and for that he is most renowned.

No one, least of all Ernie himself, would claim that he is a literary stylist like some of the men he admires and quotes. That is not his gift, but where there is a need, and few are addressing it in print, Ernie will not sit back and do nothing. Life is too short for Ernie to spend years sharpening his weapons, he must use them to vindicate God's truth, and by every biblical means spread the message. He will marshal those 'twenty-six lead soldiers'[1] and get them to serve the interests of God's kingdom. He himself says: 'I do not consider myself an author. I am more or less a compiler of what others have written. I use many books, confessions, systematics of the most respected theologians and church historians, particularly the Puritans and their successors. I resonate with what another author wrote: "I have culled a bouquet of varied flowers from other men's gardens, and nothing is my own but the string that binds them."'

Today's Evangelism: Its Message and Methods was written not because the church lacks sufficient materials on the subject of evangelism, but because most of that material concentrates on methods, or on how to stir up zeal for evangelism. There is much less in print that gives a biblical examination of the message and methods. This particular book deals more with the God-ward side of the gospel than with human responsibility, because Ernie judged that to be one of the main deficiencies in contemporary evangelism. An acquaintance of Ernie's who was also a pastor once invited a rather superficial evangelist to take a campaign in his church, and he approached Ernie to see whether he would join with him in supporting the meetings. Ernie was unhappy to identify with the proposed 'crusade', and he sought to explain his refusal to his friend. This book is that *apologia* at length. There were sixty-eight supposed conversions during that week of meetings, but in less than a month not one of them could be found. Why does this familiar pattern of events occur? What

[1] See also p. 239.

poor evangelism is everywhere, producing decisions but not disciples. It makes the spectator ask whether there is anything to claims of someone being converted. There must be something faulty at the very heart of the whole approach for contemporary evangelism to fail so appallingly and repeatedly. The book explains the reasons why Ernie (who has seen so many people come to a personal knowledge of God) deplores much of what passes under the name 'evangelism' today, and stands apart from it because there is something far better. The book also suggests the evangelistic pattern of the New Testament.

Today's Evangelism reflects the wealth of his own experience and the help he has gained from certain men, both contemporary and from church history. For example, Ernie vividly explains these intriguing words of the psalmist, 'Thy people shall be willing in the day of thy power" (*Psa.* 110:3) by this illustration:

'I remember hearing an old country preacher pick his guitar and sing a kind of 'hillbilly' song, though I'm sure he did not understand the great theological truth that the song clearly sets forth, that is, that God makes man willing. I'll call it the 'Hornet Song':

> When the Canaanites hardened their hearts against God,
> And grieved Him because of their sin,
> God sent along hornets to bring them to terms,
> And to help His own people to win.
>
> If a nest of live hornets were brought to this room,
> And the creatures allowed to go free,
> You wouldn't need urging to make yourself scarce,
> You'd want to get out, don't you see?

They wouldn't lay hold and by force of their strength
Throw you from the window, oh, no!
They wouldn't compel you to go 'gainst your will,
They'd just make you willing to go.

When Jonah was sent to the work of the Lord,
The outlook was not very bright.
He never had done such a hard thing before,
He backed off and ran from the fight.

Now, the Lord sent a great fish to swallow him up,
The story I'm sure you all know.
God did not compel him to go 'gainst his will,
He just made him willing to go.

CHORUS:

God doesn't compel us to go, oh, no, no!
He never compels us to go.
God doesn't compel us to go 'gainst our wills,
He just makes us willing to go.'

Ernie explains why he disapproves of the so-called 'altar call', that is, inviting people to get out of their seats and come to the front. He lists four reasons why this device should be discarded by anyone who longs for men and women to experience true conversion:

'There are four dangers of this man-made, Pelagian system:

1. It conveys to sinners a condition of salvation that is not in the Bible and was never practised or approved by Christ and His apostles.

2. To call sinners to the front of a church is not a divine command, but many times those who don't go forward are led to believe that they are not obeying the Spirit, and therefore, not obeying God. This is false, psychological guilt because no such thing was ever commanded by God. On the other hand, those who do go forward are often commended and are led to believe that they did something commendable, when, in many cases, they have only added to their religious deception.

3. This unbiblical system has produced the greatest record of false statistics ever compiled by church or business.

4. This system has spawned the error of representing faith in Christ as something physical to be done in order to salvation.'

Ernest Reisinger made a memorable visit to Reformed Theological Seminary, Jackson, Mississippi (RTS), in December 1970. That institution was then in its early years, and Ernie spoke on evangelism at the morning chapel services for a week. A few months earlier Walter Chantry's *Today's Gospel* (Banner of Truth) had been printed and Ernie arrived with boxes of this book and a number of others to give away.

The week began inauspiciously when he was having breakfast with Sam Patterson, the president of the Seminary. Dr Patterson, though a conservative member of the Southern Presbyterian Church, had at that time not been exposed to the radical examination of evangelism coming from such men as Lloyd-Jones, Murray, Packer and Chantry. Over breakfast he grumbled to Ernie about the dangers posed by 'theology' and 'doctrine' to evangelism. Ernie returned to his room not knowing what to do. He cried to God for help, and looked over his notes, and launched out that day in his weakness.

The impact those talks made on the students of RTS was substantial. Some of the future conservative leaders of the Presbyterian Church in America (PCA), men who would launch the Reformed University Fellowship (a growing campus outreach), had their eyes opened and could see the issues as Ernie was helped to present them. Sam Patterson's whole outlook changed. Dr Morton Smith, the professor of theology, was thrilled with all he heard and wrote appreciatively to Ernie. Men today, such as President Joseph A. Pipa, Jr. of Greenville Seminary, and others in influential pulpits, look back to that week at Reformed Seminary as the crucial period in their studies there. What Ernie taught them about evangelism has been one of the foundations for their convictions and practice.

Ford Williams, a PCA pastor in Memphis, writes:

'I well remember his speaking in chapel. His visit is actually one of the things I remember most about seminary. I had grown up in a Presbyterian Church with good Biblical preaching and teaching since the age of nine. I had taken courses ('Introduction to Reformed Theology' and 'Systematic Theology') at RTS from Morton Smith. I had heard good Reformed teaching in church and in Seminary, but, when Ernie Reisinger spoke, it was as if I were hearing it for the first time. I suppose the doctrines which he espoused were beginning to take root in my mind. I remember feeling rather agitated as I listened, and certainly afterwards. Since I had been involved in Campus Crusade for Christ during college and almost went on Crusade staff, having gone through the Institute of Biblical Studies and two weeks of staff training in California the summer I entered seminary, I naturally heard things in the aforementioned classes with which I had trouble. I had actually taken a group of high school students for the one-week high school Campus Crusade conference at Arrowhead Springs the summer before my senior year of seminary. It was as if, however, when Ernie Reisinger spoke, my quest for aligning what I had heard in college with God's truth became all the more difficult.

'I recall not really liking what I heard, yet, knowing that I couldn't let it drop. I had to deal with it. Ernie kindly gave each seminary student five free books: Alleine's *Alarm to the Unconverted*, Guthrie's *The Christian's Great Interest*, Packer's *Evangelism and the Sovereignty of God*, Chantry's *Today's Gospel*, and Kuiper's *God-Centered Evangelism*. Soon after he spoke, I was talking with a fellow student about my concerns regarding his message. I even remember feeling Ernie was being a little harsh and cold, though, as I look back, it was more likely my trying to deal with his message rather than his manner.

'I felt I needed to read one of those books. "Where should I start?" was my question to my friend. He suggested *Evangelism and the Sovereignty of God*. I took his recommendation. I read Packer, and then Chantry's book. I didn't come to fully embrace these wonderful doctrines of grace as my own immediately, but Reisinger's visit was surely a major rung on the ladder to that prize.

'It wasn't too long after that that I began to see through what I had been taught in college. I took another group of high school students to Arrowhead Springs that summer. On this visit, things began to make sense so much so that, as I began my first year of ministry to college students a few weeks later, our first study book was the Packer book. I still think it is an excellent place to begin teaching the truths of the Reformed faith to those who do not understand or agree.

'I wish that I had thought to get Ernie to autograph each of those five books, for I still appreciate his generous gift. But, all the more do I appreciate his willingness to speak of the true things of God and his Word so strongly that it disturbed my thinking to the extent that I soon began to change. What a blessing! How I love the truth that he imparted. How I want others to know it and to love it too, not only because it's truth, but also because it is so dear to the heart of those who understand it.

'I often think of a dear student friend Dean Hall. We were attending the Philadelphia Conference on Reformed Theology at Independent Presbyterian Church in Memphis. The theme that year was 'Predestination'. Dr Packer was giving the opening message. At its conclusion Dean looked at me and whispered, "But, Ford, why me? Why me?" Soon afterward we sang:

And can it be, that I should gain
An interest in the Saviour's blood?

What a moment that was!'

While Ernie was pastor of North Pompano Baptist Church he wrote a hard-hitting 24-page booklet entitled, *What Should We Think of the Carnal Christian*? (Banner of Truth, 1978). It analyses one of the major problems in the contemporary evangelical scene in the United States. If evangelicals are now 35 or 40 million strong, how is it that the *life* of the nation is so little affected? Evangelism has reaped a great harvest but the question has been rightly raised, what is wrong with the harvest? One of the most popular answers to this question is that too many Christians have stopped at 'conversion': they are so-called 'carnal Christians' who have not yet learned to live a surrendered life. Ernie examines that theory and its misuse of the opening verses of 1 Corinthians 3:1–4 where Paul writes, 'And I, brethren, could not speak unto you as unto spiritual, but as unto carnal, even as unto babes in Christ . . . are ye not carnal?'

Ernie charges that the proponents of the 'carnal Christian' theory separate the two blessings of the new covenant, that of experiencing the forgiveness of sins and of having a new heart (and the new life that flows from it), making a second work of grace essential. They also hold the possibility of having Christ as Saviour while rejecting his Lordship.

Herbert W. Epp is the son of Theodore Epp of the Good News Broadcasting Association. Theodore died in 1985 after forty-five years of a most influential radio ministry, the *Back to the Bible* broadcast, which was transmitted from more than six hundred stations. Ernie spent some time with Herbert W. Epp in Omaha in 1980. Epp read *What Should We Think of the Carnal Christian?* and said to Ernie:

'For some years I have felt that the doctrine of the carnal Christian, as popularly taught, had problems in it, since my reading of Scripture has led me to be unable to separate salvation from discipleship, and Christ as Savior from Christ as Lord. What your booklet did for me was to bring together a number of additional matters relating to this subject, particularly a new look at 1 Corinthians 3, to see that carnality is a condition of the Christian relating to the exercise of certain aspects of the sin-principle that dwells in him, and not a special class of people – which opens the door for perversions of the gospel. I really had no criticisms of the booklet. I was helped by it.

'You might be interested that we had had some discussion and differences with some here at the Broadcast on this subject. When I was up-dating the doctrinal statement of the Broadcast in conjunction with my father, I always spoke of our obligation to receive Christ as Lord and Savior. Some objected, saying that the lordship of Christ should be treated under the heading of the Christian Life rather than Salvation. I objected to this, and was gratified that my father insisted with me that we retain the lordship of Christ in the Salvation section.'

Other pamphlets and booklets came from Ernie's pen during the 1980s, a number of which were first published in the *Founders' Journal*. In Cape Coral in the early 1990s Ernie made a contribution to the so-called 'lordship controversy'. John MacArthur had written a book entitled *The Gospel According to Jesus* which challenged the theory that one could receive Jesus' salvation with all its benefits yet refuse to have him as one's Lord. Such ideas are very common. It is a widespread notion in Russian and eastern European Christianity. That someone like MacArthur, considered one of their best and brightest leaders, should have rejected this idea so trenchantly and in print shocked many.

Books written in opposition to MacArthur included Robert Lightner's *The Savior, Sin, and Salvation*, Charles Ryrie's *So Great Salvation*, and Zane C. Hodges' books, *The Gospel Under Siege* and *Absolutely Free!*, while books supporting John MacArthur included Kenneth L. Gentry, Jr.'s *Lord of the Saved*, a book edited by Michael S. Horton, *Christ the Lord*, and Richard P. Belcher's *A Layman's Guide to the Lordship Controversy*. It was invigorating to find a theological issue of such importance coming into the public square and turning many people to their Bibles. Not since J. I. Packer wrote an introduction to John Owen's *The Death of Death in the Death of Christ* (Banner of Truth) thirty years earlier had the correspondence columns of certain religious papers buzzed with matters of doctrine and exegesis. The letters were coming from people who tended to say, 'Don't talk theology to me, just tell me about Jesus.' When the Spirit of God is poured out on the church, such periods are always characterized by serious theological discussion. It was so during the Reformation, in the Puritan period during the following century, and throughout the Great Awakening. In fact one mark of the blessed Spirit's absence from the twentieth-century church was the decline of interest in theology.

In the quarterly *Founders' Journal* Ernie wrote a series of articles on the lordship debate taking his readers back to the notes of the Scofield Bible, but way beyond them to the Marrow Controversy and the Sandemanianism of the eighteenth century. He demonstrated that the twentieth century's denial of Christ's Lordship over his own sheep was nothing new. What goes around comes round. The possibility of forgiven, redeemed sinners living like free spirits *outside* the sovereign rule and protection of their Saviour was an old error with a new dress. But in our age the requirements for what is judged to be a 'saving confession of faith' have become astonishingly little – a raising of a hand, a walk to the front of a meeting, or the 'Amen' at the end of another's brief prayer of thanks to Jesus for dying on the cross for us. Wesley's preachers had far higher views of saving faith than that. Today Zane C. Hodges affirms, 'God's love can embrace sinful people unconditionally, with *no binding requirements attached at all.*' Salvation, he says, involves '*no spiritual commitment whatsoever.*'[1]

[1] Hodges, *The Gospel Under Siege* (Dallas: Redención Viva, 1981), p. 14.

An experienced campaigner like Ernest Reisinger had his own contribution to make, and thus he produced, in 1994, *Lord and Christ* (Presbyterian and Reformed Publishing [P&R], 178 pp.). John MacArthur wrote appreciatively. Dr J. I. Packer also wrote to Ernie. He had once dubbed Ernie 'everyone's favourite uncle'! When he received a copy of *Lord and Christ* he wrote this letter:

'Dear Ernie,

I have been sent a copy of *Lord and Christ*. I read it through. I found it delightful – so clear, so strong, and so honouring to our Lord Jesus. Thank you for writing it, and I hope it sells well. Of all the anti-anti-Lordship books it is the one I shall now recommend.

I hope you are well in body (I'm sure you are in heart) – last time we had contact you were labouring a bit, as I recall. God is good to Kit and me in that way. I don't feel my age and when I retire (at 70, next year) it looks as if I shall still have energy for more heavy writing that I hope to do. Meanwhile, Regent grows and prospers, which is a further matter for joy. I am able to ensure that Regent's theology has a Reformed cast.

God bless you, Ernie, and your lady, as the years go by.

Yours in God's grace,

Jim.'

Three years later another book of Reisinger's appeared under the title, *The Law and the Gospel* (P & R, 1997, 196 pp.). A statement made in his hearing had a profound influence upon Ernie, fuelling a desire to know the relationship between the Ten Commandments (the Moral Law) and the gospel of Christ. The speaker was an old Southern Baptist evangelist, now dead, who said, 'The first message of the cross is the law of God.' Christ was born under the law, lived under its obligations throughout his life, and bore the curse of the broken law in his own body on the tree. Ernie has spent many years seeking to understand the relationship between the law and the gospel, and this book was the fruit of his labours. Two years later (1999) the Banner of Truth published a slimmer book by him on the same theme entitled *Whatever Happened to the Ten Commandments*? In this book Ernie gathers together verses from all over the Bible on each of the Ten Commandments, and explains the duties required and sins forbidden.

But Ernie's pen had not yet run dry. In the year 2000, D. Matthew Allen and he wrote a book entitled *A Quiet Reformation: A Chronicle of Beginnings of Reformation in the Southern Baptist Convention* (Founders' Press, P. O. Box 150931, Cape Coral, FL 33915). The book summarizes the need for reformation, and the beginnings of reform in the SBC. It gives encouragement and instruction in local church reformation. It is a valuable history of the events of the last twenty years of the twentieth century relating to Christian witness within the Convention, and for their friends everywhere. Hot on the heels of this book appeared two more pamphlets, *Will Calvinism Kill Evangelism?* and *A Southern Baptist Looks at the Biblical Doctrine of Election* (Founders' Press).

Ernest Reisinger's attitude to literature is well summed up in his little tract, *Twenty-Six Soldiers*, which is worthy of being quoted at length:

'I hope I have encouraged you to use good sound literature in your ministry. There is power in those twenty-six soldiers – the letters of our alphabet upon the printed page.

'Francis Bacon said, "If I might control the literature of the household, I would guarantee the well-being of the church and state."

'Martin Luther said, "We must throw the printer's inkpot at the devil."

'Robert Murray M'Cheyne said, "The smallest tract may be the Stone in David's sling. In the hands of Christ it may bring down a giant soul."

'August Schlegel said, "Literature is the immortality of speech."

'John Trapp said, "Be careful what books you read, for as water tastes of the soil it runs through, so does the soul taste of the authors that a man reads."

'Samuel Zwemmer said, "No other agency can penetrate so deeply, witness so daringly, abide so persistently and influence so irresistibly as the printed page."

'The printed page never flinches, it never shows cowardice; it is never tempted to compromise. The printed page never gets tired; it never gets disheartened.

'The printed page travels cheaply – you can be a missionary for the price of a stamp. It requires no buildings in which to operate.

'The printed page works while you sleep. It never loses its temper in discussion. And it works when you are gone from the scene.

'The printed page is a visitor that gets inside the home and stays there. It always catches a man in the right mood, it speaks to him only when he is reading it.

'It never answers back and it sticks to the point.

'There are some principles in using literature in your ministry that will be helpful:

1. Know the books you give to others.
2. Know the person, his needs and capacity, to whom you intend to give a book.

3. Know the most serious areas of ignorance and the errors of our day. (The doctor does not give green pills to everyone, and he does not give medicine that is not relevant to what he believes to be the problem.)

4. Do not be afraid to invest some money in your own missionary project.

5. Follow through with other books and with discussion on subjects in the books you use.

6. Aim to have a book-table in your church and see that its appearance is varied from week to week.

7. Be sure to use books and literature that are consistent with the teaching of the Bible.

8. Soak all the books you distribute in fervent prayer.'

For some of the thoughts expressed above Ernie was indebted to D. M. Panton, whose words about the printed page he would often quote:

'It never flinches, never shows cowardice; it is never tempted to compromise; it never tires, never grows disheartened; it travels cheaply, and requires no hired hall; it works while we sleep; it never loses its temper, and it works long after we are dead. The printed page is a visitor which gets inside the home and stays there; it always catches a man in the right mood, for it speaks to him only when he is reading it; it always sticks to what is said, and never answers back; and it is bait left permanently in the pool.'

24

STILL IN THE LAND OF THE DYING

When the nineteenth-century black preacher, Andrew Marshall, was old and infirm, some neighbours were going to visit old acquaintances of his in the northern states. 'Tell them', said Marshall, 'that I am yet in the land of the *dying,* but am bound for the land of the living. There is no death there, while all things are dying here.' So it is today with Ernest C. Reisinger. In 1985, after eight years at North Pompano Baptist Church, he resigned once and for all from that pastorate. He was in his sixty-sixth year and Mima and he had long determined to settle down back in Cape Coral near Duke and Katie Irwin's home. It was Katie who had said to Duke thirty-five years earlier, 'Now I don't want you to become a religious fanatic like Ernie Reisinger.' Not long after those words were spoken they both had come to know for themselves the God whom Ernie served and the two families spent their last decades living near to one another.

But his close links with a local church were not ended. It was on a visit to the Irwins that he noticed a little sign on the side of a road announcing *Grace Baptist Church*. They are happy words for him, and the Reisingers attended the church for several Sundays. Ernie gave to the minister a copy of Dr Lloyd-Jones's *Preaching and Preachers* before flying to Scotland for a Banner of Truth trustees' meeting. When he called Mima from Edinburgh to find out what kind of Sunday she had experienced at Grace Baptist Church she replied dejectedly, 'You'll never believe what happened in the church this Sunday. They fired the preacher on the spot!' By the time he returned home from Scotland the minister had moved out of his study and removed all his possessions. Ernie was never to see him again. Ernie soon discovered that in the church's three-year existence the congregation had gone through two major splits.

Before long Ernie was asked to preach and soon he was approached to become their pastor. Though he had already retired three times and was weary he agreed to become an interim pastor. The congregation of Grace Baptist Church were a pleasant enough people, but doctrinally deficient and lacking leaders who met New Testament standards. The church was more like a religious social club with a congenial atmosphere than an assembly of God. Few of the congregation had any understanding of the basic truths of Christianity. Several candidates came and preached but were either unsuitable or unwilling to instruct a fellowship with such limited grasp of the faith. For example, one Ronald Metzger preached there, and he wrote Ernie a letter on 10 March 1986 that mirrored Ernie's own assessment:

'I hope that the Grace Baptist Church will make some positive changes in its leadership and its Constitution and By-laws. There is no way that any good pastor would be able to do the Lord's work under that present system. So I will be praying that God will use you to help in bringing about some needed changes in that ministry to prepare the way for a new minister.'

At this juncture Ernie's mind went back to that day of prayer spent in a Holiday Inn near Dallas on 13 November 1982 with Fred Malone, Tom Nettles and the brothers, Bill and Tom Ascol. Five years later Tom Ascol was completing his doctorate at Southwestern Seminary, and in June 1987 Ernie commended him to the Cape Coral church. The congregation called him without one dissenting vote, and Ernie was invited to be his unsalaried associate.

The work of personal evangelism continued as naturally and faithfully as ever. Mack M. Tomlinson once visited Ernie and, after they had breakfasted together, Ernie said to him, 'Hey, let's go next door and see some friends of mine, a businessman and his wife, and give them this booklet. I've been witnessing to them for a while and I think I have their ear.' He had already given them some material on the Ten Commandments. They received a genuinely warm reception from this family who turned out to be Muslims. They were delighted to see Ernie and his friend and promptly took the gospel material which he offered. Ernie did not say much, but it was not necessary. A warm smile and loving simple words won the moment. Tomlinson says, 'Walking out, I knew that such encounters had occurred hundreds of times. This is how he has lived his Christian life, and it is his concern to see others do the same.'

Few ministers know Ernie as well as Walter Chantry, and he makes a wise assessment of someone who is his spiritual father:

'Many have a desire to serve the Lord. Ernie has the gift of turning that desire into concrete, manageable church-oriented projects. He has never lost sight of the fact that very great movements of God's Spirit begin with small steps. He has realized and helped others to realize that he who is faithful in little things will eventually be entrusted by the Lord with wider responsibilities. Ernie never despises little things – a prayer time with one other person, a Bible reading to a student, a one-to-one discussion, a book given, a word of testimony; to him these were seeds to plant or bread to cast upon the waters. Not all of the seeds germinated. Not all of the bread returned dividends, but many great oaks have sprung up and large shiploads of cargo have returned from small efforts performed with faithful devotion to the Lord.'

The work of reformation in Grace Baptist Church, Cape Coral, was soon gathering momentum and expository preaching and teaching had been introduced. A book table had been set up, and Tom Ascol gave this side of the church's ministry a new momentum. The key members had received many books, devotional books like *Praying Always* by Frans Bakker, *The Still Hour* by Austin Phelps, and Spurgeon's *Morning and Evening*, but also doctrinal literature like J. I. Packer's *Evangelism and the Sovereignty of God*, John MacArthur's *Ashamed of the Gospel*, Iain Murray's *The Forgotten Spurgeon*, Tom Nettles' *A Foundation for the Future*, and John Dagg's *Manual of Theology*.

Reading clubs were launched where a 'book of the month' was selected, read and then discussed. Books were used to help the adult Bible studies on Sunday mornings, such as Don Whitney's *Spiritual Disciplines for the Christian Life* and *Spiritual Disciplines in the Church*, John Piper's *Let the Nations Be Glad*, and J. I. Packer's *Knowing God* and *God's Words*. Ernie's own *Today's Evangelism* was widely distributed in the congregation. Members were encouraged to give away books in ministry. P. B. Power's *Book of Comfort* and J. C. Ryle's *Sickness* have been left beside countless sickbeds. Over seven hundred copies of Jerry Bridges' *Trusting God, Even When Life Hurts* have been distributed. That has been the all-time favourite book for members to give away. They gave this title to dozens of pastors who themselves, or whose congregations, had lost their homes and libraries to Hurricane Andrew in 1992.

The pastors in the local Baptist Association also received books from the church, including Ernie's own as they were published. At fairs, parades and local residences Christian booklets and even books which explain the Christian faith are regularly given away. Around the world missionaries, congregations and pastors are sent helpful books and cassettes. At Christmas, other gifts may be sent to these pastors and their wives. After Tom Ascol had served in Cape Coral for one year he informed the congregation that more than two thousand books and booklets had been distributed in those months. The church does all it can by a literature ministry to bring men, women, boys and girls to a saving knowledge of the Lord Jesus, and to help Christians grow in an understanding of their faith. But it is through his long pastorate, gracious manner and happy family life that Tom Ascol has exemplified the grace of the doctrines which he preaches.

A stable and united spiritual home for himself and Mima, with Don and his wife Barbara, has been an inexpressible comfort to them all through the challenges of their advancing years. Each week they anticipate gathering with the Lord's people and finding strength by the means of grace. John Bunyan warned each Christian that on the journey between the City of Destruction and the Celestial City the Hill

Difficulty has to be climbed. So the Reisingers have found it, as Mima's health and Ernie's own have become increasingly precarious.

Serious physical difficulties began on 12 February 1990 when Ernie went completely blind in his left eye. Mima had two serious back operations, one just below her neck. Both were successful. She broke her foot, and later her wrist. Mima has had a total of eleven operations in her life, most of them major surgery. But the worst trial of all came in December 1996. On 10 December Ernie was taken to the emergency room and within two days had serious surgery. Ten days later he was discharged, but on the next day it was Mima who had to visit the emergency room. Don called from the hospital to inform his father that brain surgery was her only hope, and even that was very uncertain. To operate or not to operate? The surgeon was asked: if it had been his mother or wife, what would be his decision? He gave an unequivocal answer – Operate. On Christmas Day 1996 the surgery took place. It was neither straightforward nor wholly successful. A stroke occurred and, for four months, gentle loving Mima could swallow neither food nor liquid. She was fed by a tube in her side, and it has resulted in her being unable to walk or stand alone again. Later she even broke her hip, which required another operation.

Yet Mima gives her love and receives in response wonderful care from the family. She has not lost her sense of humour. Don and Barbara look after her during the day and Ernie at night. She is uncomplaining, and in her last years has appeared more confident and cheerful than ever, attending church each Sunday and continuing discerning concerning the sermons she hears. Mima loves to hear much about the Lord Jesus Christ in a sermon. Christ's grace is proving sufficient for them all. Woven into Don's labours in his Christian literature outreach is his presence to help Mom when she needs him. Barbara serves as one of the secretaries at Grace Baptist Church. The family knows that earth has no sorrows that heaven cannot heal.

Between January 1994 and October 1996 ten thousand books and pamphlets were mailed out from the Reisingers' home. That needed many trips to the Post Office! The year 1990 saw the largest distribution of over eight thousand books and pamphlets throughout the world. This ministry headed by Don prompts hundreds of letters. The *Christian Gospel Foundation* flourishes, though no longer subsidized, since the construction company is no longer in business.

On 10 November 1998, Walter Chantry wrote to Ernie from Grace Baptist Church in Carlisle. For a year they had been building a 600-seat auditorium and making some changes to their premises which contain Sunday School rooms and a Christian School (started in 1968). The cost ran to over two million dollars. The church had come a long way since those ten families had covenanted together under Ernie's leadership on 9 December 1951 to commence an uncompromised evangelical testimony in Carlisle. The church today has more than 250 members. It has contributed over four million dollars to missions in the last forty years. In his letter Chantry told Ernie:

'We plan to have formal dedication services on Sunday, December 5th 1999. This will coincide with our congregation's 48th anniversary. Would you be willing to come to Carlisle and preach on that occasion? Our Board of Elders can think of no one we would rather have preach the Word on that day. We would love to have Mima come along if that is possible. She is included in all of the above invitation, but the preaching. She too is precious to us at Grace Church.'

'It is the dearest spot on earth to me', Ernie told the congregation when he had journeyed to Carlisle and fulfilled this his last engagement to preach. 'I don't have words to express my feelings. You could easily get someone more qualified, but not one more grateful.' His two texts for the occasion were, 'Those who sow in tears shall reap in joy. He who continually goes forth weeping, bearing seed for sowing, shall doubtless come again rejoicing, bringing his sheaves with him' (*Psa.* 126:5–6), and 'Return and tell Hezekiah the leader of my people, Thus says the LORD, the God of David your father, I have heard your prayer, I have seen your tears; surely I will heal you. On the third day you shall go up to the house of the LORD' (*2 Kings* 20:5).

On this occasion Ernie recalled the beginning of the work, as they were confronting the perplexity and rumours of Carlisle's citizens: 'One person stopped one of my employees and asked if it were true that Reisinger takes 10 percent off everyone's wages and puts it in his church!'

From some observations of William Jay of Bath he exhorted them:

1. Do not look for something in the law which can only be found in the gospel.
2. Do not look in yourself for what can only be found in Christ.
3. Do not look in your fellow creatures for what is only found in the Creator.
4. Do not look on earth for what is to be found in heaven.

The theme of Ernie's sermon was the heartfelt grief of the Christian for the world. He declared:

'As long as you are sincerely committed to prayer and the souls of men, you will never hear our Lord say to you what he once said to the church of Laodicea. You remember that they were saying of themselves, "We are rich, have become wealthy, and have need of nothing." But the Lord Jesus had a different opinion, saying to them, "You are wretched, miserable, poor, blind and naked." If you are sincerely and deeply interested in men's souls you will never become a religious social club or begin to depend upon Hollywood tactics.

'In I Samuel 7 we have the celebration of a victory over the Philistines. The prophet Samuel lays a victory stone between Mizpeh and Shen, and calls the name of it Ebenezer, saying, "Hitherto hath the LORD helped us" (*1 Sam*. 7:12). Surely we can say this too. We have a distance to go, a few more trials, a few more joys like today, a few more temptations, a few more triumphs, a few more hardships, a few more victories, more deep waters and more high mountains. Then comes old age, sickness, disease and death. But that is not the end. No! No! We will raise one more Ebenezer stone when we get to that river that has no bridge and then we will shout, "Ebenezer, hitherto has the Lord helped us!" Be sure, be very sure, the Lord who has helped us so far will help us to the end. "I will never leave thee nor forsake thee." O Christian, have courage as we pile the stones for the future. "Hitherto hath the LORD helped us."

'I know of no better way of celebrating this our Ebenezer Day than by raising the marriage ring of Christ and being joined to him for ever and ever. This will be my last invitation to you to trust him as your Savior and bow to him as your

Lord. Oh, I can't give you a formula as to what it means to come to Christ, but listen carefully. The best I can do is to tell you what is involved in coming to Christ: See your spiritual need because of your sin! See how suitable a Saviour Christ is to meet all your needs! Commit yourself to him without reservation as the only one who can meet your need.

'If you have not experienced those three things then my parting word to you is, Sinner, give the Lord no rest until he sends out that Spirit whom he promised to give those who ask, that Spirit who convicts and gives sight to the blind and life to the dead. Oh, give him no rest until he causes you to know that which belongs to your everlasting peace and brings you to your duty.'

Tears formed an appropriate theme for Ernie's final sermon, as numbers wept like those on the quayside of Ephesus as they heard the apostle Paul's farewell address. 'What grieved them most was his statement that they would never see his face again.' (*Acts* 20:38)

Ernest and Mima Reisinger are now waiting on the bank of that river that has no bridge – as John Bunyan described death. Ernie's funeral hymn has been chosen. It will consist of some of the stanzas of this hymn of Anne R. Cousin's *Immanuel's Land*, which is based on many extracts from Samuel Rutherford's letters:

The sands of time are sinking,
  The dawn of Heaven breaks,
The summer morn I've sighed for,
  The fair sweet morn awakes:
Dark, dark hath been the midnight,
  But dayspring is at hand,

And glory, glory dwelleth
In Immanuel's land.

Ernest Reisinger has composed his last will and testament, and here are some relevant paragraphs from it:

'I commit my soul into the hands of the only Saviour of poor lost sinners. And being such, I cast myself on His mercy and rest on His promise to present my soul spotless before the Throne of my Heavenly Father, as His purchased possession.

'I pray that all my family would seek a saving interest in the person and work of Christ, for with that they would be rich though I did not leave them a penny; without that they would be poor, had I left them the whole world. I entreat my loved ones remaining to maintain and defend the Christian faith at any cost of personal sacrifice.

'I want to leave my family and all who have read these words with three questions:

1. What is the only safe ground of a sinner's hope?
2. How does that only safe ground become the ground of my own hope?
3. How am I to know that the only safe ground has become, and continues to be the ground of my hope, so that I may be assured that my hope is not "the hope of the hypocrite" that shall perish but the "hope that maketh not ashamed"?

'Each has its own answer. Be sure not to confuse the answer of one of them for the answer of either of the others.

1. The only safe ground of the sinner's hope is the sovereign mercy of God, exercised in consistency with his righteousness,

through the atoning sacrifice of His Son, made known to us in the gospel revelation.

2. The only way in which this only safe ground of hope can become the ground of my hope is by believing the word of the truth of the gospel.

3. And the only way in which I can obtain permanent, satisfactory evidence, that the only safe ground of hope has become the ground of my own hope is by continuing to believe the Gospel, and by living under the influence of the Gospel believed.'

It is fitting to give the last word to Ernest Reisinger himself.

'As I stand on the bank of the river I do not know the time of my departure, yet it is unalterably fixed by my Heavenly Father, He fixes it wisely and lovingly. He sends the messenger. His time to call me is my time to go. I want to take three last looks:

1. First, A look back. I have many mixed feelings looking back. There is a feeling of deep gratitude, a thankful look: thankful to God for a full life of joy in serving the King of kings; thankful for a wonderful sixty years married to a wonderful wife; thankful for Christian friends who have encouraged me, corrected me, patiently taught me; thankful for the good providence of sending Christian teachers across my path to instruct me in the great doctrines of the Christian faith. In looking back, I am sorry for the many mistakes, for many words not spoken in love, for impatience with my family and sometimes people in the church. I am thankful that there is mercy and forgiveness.

2. Second, a look around, with a keen interest in the mission that has occupied my life in carrying out our Lord's clearest command: "Go ye into all the world and preach the Gospel," to spread his truth in the earth (*Psa.* 145:10–12). It is painful to think that many of my fellow creatures have never heard of God's salvation, never heard of our Lord Jesus Christ.

3. Third, a look forward with sweet assurance that my Saviour will keep his promise, "I go to prepare a place for you." And though heaven is to be considered more as a state than a place, and though even now our happiness does not depend essentially upon local situations, yet these have their importance. And what beautiful and enchanting places have we seen and heard of and imagined. But, "Eye hath not seen, nor ear heard, neither have entered into the heart of man, the things which God hath prepared for them that love him." What a residence was Eden before the fall of the first Adam! But even Eden in its unfallen glory fell infinitely short of the excellency of the abode of the second Adam, the Lord from Heaven:

Oh, the delights, the heavenly joys,
The glories of the place,
Where Jesus sheds the brightest beams
Of his o'erflowing grace!

'I look to that promise, not as a profitable servant but as a pardoned sinner. One phrase could summarize my autobiography – "A debtor to mercy alone".

'My Prayer is: "Lord, assure me that you will be with me

for my last journey, and that, at the end of this valley of tears, I shall enter Immanuel's Land."

'I would have engraved on my gravestone these words, "He did what he could."'

INDEX OF AUTHORS AND TITLES

GENERAL INDEX

Since the whole book is about Ernest Reisinger, only a few entries are included under his name in this index.